MIND OVER MUSCLE

Unleashing the Hidden Power of Young Athletes

RAPOLAS JANONIS

CONTENTS

INTRODUCTION TO DEVELOPMENTAL PSYCHOLOGY IN SPORTS

DEFINING DEVELOPMENTAL PSYCHOLOGY

At its heart, developmental psychology is all about understanding the journey of individuals as they grow, evolve, and navigate the complexities of life. This field delves into various domains—cognitive, emotional, social, and physical development—that are intricately woven together, illuminating how these experiences shape our behaviors and interactions. When we apply these principles to sports, it becomes clear that grasping the nuances of development is essential for nurturing young athletes, both on the playing field and in their everyday lives.

Consider Piaget's theory of cognitive development, which outlines the distinct stages children and teenagers pass through as they refine their thinking and comprehension of the world around them. For young athletes, these stages manifest in their growing understanding of game strategies and their ability to analyze performance. Some might quickly grasp the intricacies of a play, while others might need more time to connect the dots.

Meanwhile, Erikson's exploration of emotional and social development reveals just how significant these factors are in shaping a young athlete's resilience. The ability to cope with the pressures of competition, manage stress, and navigate relationships with peers and coaches can profoundly impact performance. It's a fine balance—one that can either bolster an athlete's drive and success or, if overlooked, hinder their progress.

By weaving together these developmental threads, we gain a richer understanding of what it takes to cultivate not just skilled athletes but well-rounded individuals ready to tackle the challenges both on and off the field.

IMPORTANCE OF AGE AND STAGE

In the world of youth sports, the age and developmental stage of young athletes are like the secret ingredients that influence their motivations, performances, and emotional health. Childhood is often depicted as a vibrant time filled with exploration and the thrill of learning new skills, a period where kids are driven by an inborn love for play and the joy of the game. Studies have shown that young children who engage in sports mainly for the fun of it tend to display greater enthusiasm and resilience, which often leads to a more fulfilling experience with less risk of burnout (Couts, 2019). It's these carefree moments on the field or court that fuel their spirits and shape their love for the sport, laying a foundation for lifelong engagement and well-being.

On the flip side, teenage years bring a whirlwind of psychological and physical transformations. For teen athletes, these changes can feel particularly intense. They often find themselves under pressure from every direction, grappling with the unwelcome notion that their value is tied to how well they perform on the field. This struggle to balance expectations can blur the lines between self-worth and athletic achievement, making the journey even more challenging. Consider the story of Mia, a 14-year-old soccer player who once relished the thrill of the game but began feeling overwhelmed by the expectations of winning championships.

Mia had always loved the feel of the grass beneath her cleats, the rush of the wind in her hair as she sprinted down the field, and the satisfying sound of her foot connecting with the ball. At 14, soccer was more than just a game; it was a source of joy and freedom, a world where she could be herself—a girl laughing with friends, racing towards goalposts, carefree in the moment. But as her team started to climb the ranks, something changed. The playful banter between teammates faded, replaced by hushed conversations filled with talk of championships and stats.

As the stakes got higher, so did the pressure. What had once been pure joy transformed into a weight pulling her down, a tightness in her chest that made it hard to focus. Mia found herself lying awake at night, grappling with expectations that felt impossible to meet. The thrill of a well-timed pass became overshadowed by anxiety; each game morphed into a test, a performance review where she was her harshest critic.

One Saturday, standing on the sidelines before an important match, Mia watched her friends warm up, their laughter a distant echo in her mind. The fear of disappointing her teammates loomed over her like a dark cloud, and she could barely breathe, trapped between her love for sport and the pressure to succeed. Mia realized she had to find a way back to that carefree girl who played for the sheer thrill of it all, or risk losing herself in the chase for trophies that no longer felt worth the cost. In that moment, she understood the journey ahead wasn't just about soccer; it was about reclaiming her joy amidst the competing noise of expectation.

ROLE OF COACHES AND PARENTS

Coaches and parents are necessary for nurturing positive psychological development in young athletes. It's in the moments spent together on the sidelines, in the heat of practice, where the foundations of confidence and resilience are laid. A well-timed word of encouragement, a thumbs up after a tough play, or a gentle nudge towards improvement can echo in a child's mind long after the game has ended.

Imagine a coach who gathers the team not just to sharpen their running drills but to celebrate their small victories—like the way a player held their ground against a rival or the courage it took to try a new skill. It's a philosophy rooted in personal growth, one that sidesteps the relentless chase for medals and accolades in favor of cultivating a spirit of joy and discovery.

Parents, too, play their part, their cheers rising above the noise of competition, reminding their children that, win or lose, their efforts matter more than the scoreboard. They cultivate an environment where the thrill of the game, the satisfaction of learning, and the camaraderie among teammates become the true prizes. In this delicate balance between support and guidance, young athletes learn that their worth is not tethered to trophies, but rather to their journey, fostering a mentality that thrives on passion and perseverance.

Take the example of Jack, a talented swimmer.

In the energetic environment of the swimming pool, 12-year-old Jack took a deep breath, his heart pounding with a mix of excitement and nerves. Each practice felt like a tiny battle, not just against the clock but within himself. Coach Ryan, with his easy smile and calm demeanor, stood at the edge of the pool, a reassuring figure in Jack's ever-spinning world of competition.

In this tightly-knit community of parents and young athletes, the atmosphere was charged with aspirations. But amidst the rush of competition, Coach Ryan emphasized one golden rule: effort over outcome. To him, every stroke Jack swam was a step toward becoming not just a better swimmer but a more resilient person.

"Hey, Jack! Love how you focused on your breathing today," Coach Ryan called out during a brief pause in the practice, his voice warm and genuine. Jack's face lit up at the praise, a spark of pride igniting inside him. It wasn't just about the medals or the times, it was about improvement.

As summer passed, Jack began to internalize this philosophy. Rather than fixating on the scoreboard, he found joy in mastering new techniques and challenging himself in ways that felt personal and significant. When he finally looked at his finishing times, it wasn't disappointment that filled him, but a sense of achievement for how far he'd come.

This nurturing environment, crafted by Coach Ryan and supported by understanding parents, transformed the pressure of competition into a journey of self-exploration. Jack wasn't just training for a race, he was shaping his spirit, acquiring the confidence that would carry him far beyond the pool's edge. In the end, it wasn't just about being a fast swimmer; it was about becoming the best version of himself, one lap at a time.

Parents are the foundation of the emotional support system that allows young athletes to flourish. In the intricate dance of youth sports, it's those subtle gestures of encouragement that echo louder than any demanding shout from the sidelines. Research by Fredricks and Eccles (2004) highlights this dynamic, revealing that when parents foster a supportive atmosphere—one infused with warmth rather than relentless pressure—young athletes often find a deeper well of motivation. This nurturing approach not only cultivates their enthusiasm for the game but also nurtures a broader, more positive perspective on sports itself. In such an environment, the joy of play outweighs the fear of failure, allowing the love for the sport to flourish.

IMPACT OF TEAM DYNAMICS

The dynamic among teammates shapes the growth of young athletes in profound ways. When kids feel connected to one another, they not only enhance their social skills but also lift each other's spirits, creating a nurturing atmosphere that allows everyone to thrive. Being part of a team goes beyond just the game; it builds a sense of camaraderie and belonging that is vital during those formative years. Here, collaboration becomes second nature, teaching lessons that extend well beyond the field (Smith et al., 2012).

The atmosphere within a team can shape a young athlete in profound ways, acting as a backdrop for growth and discovery. In a setting where encouragement reigns and victories are celebrated together, kids can blossom, forging friendships that weave into the fabric of their identities. For instance, take Tracy, an 11-year-old who once tiptoed through practices, her self-doubt overshadowing her love for basketball. But as she joined a team that thrived on inclusivity and shared goals, she found her voice among her teammates.

No longer just a shy girl, Tracy emerged, her laughter ringing out during drills and her confidence growing with every game. The connections she cultivated with her peers acted like a safety net, catching her whenever her nerves threatened to pull her under. In this nurturing environment, her social skills sharpened and her joy for the sport flourished, illustrating how vital teamwork, mutual respect, and collective achievement can be in a young athlete's life.

All around her, the camaraderie was palpable, and each cheer from her teammates fortified not just her game, but her very sense of self. Here, in the arena of friendship and support, Tracy was no longer just an athlete; she was part of something larger, a community that helped define who she was, lifting her spirits and nurturing her emotional well-being.

IDENTIFYING DEVELOPMENTAL NEEDS

Recognizing and understanding the unique developmental needs of young athletes is imperative for fostering their growth. Mental skills training, emotional regulation, and fostering a growth mindset can be instrumental in enhancing athletes' psychological resilience. Research indicates that athletes who adopt a growth mindset, believing that their abilities can improve over time, are more likely to embrace challenges and persist through adversities (Dweck, 2006).

An example can be found in the experience of Audrey.

In the heart of a small town, where summer breezes whispered through the trees, thirteen-year-old Audrey stood at the edge of the badminton court, racket in hand. The sun warmed her back, but the heat was nothing compared to the pressure swirling inside her. She loved badminton—the way the shuttlecock danced in the air, the crack of the racket hitting the birdie—but lately, self-doubt had become a constant companion, shadowing her every move.

It was during one of her practice sessions that her coach noticed her hesitation. "Audrey," he said, his voice steady yet encouraging, "Let's try something new. We need to work on not just your swings, but how you think before you swing." With that, they began focusing on mental skills training—practices to help her regulate her emotions and build a sturdy mindset that could weather the toughest of matches.

At first, it felt strange. How could breathing exercises and positive affirmations possibly change the game? But as she learned to identify her fears and reframe them into challenges to overcome, the world of badminton started to shift for her. Each lesson became a stepping stone, each setback a lesson rather than a barrier. She began to understand the concept of a growth mindset, inspired by the idea that like her skills, her confidence could grow over time.

Weeks turned into months, and with each practice, the self-doubt that once lingered turned into a flicker of determination. At the local tournament, she found herself facing off against a tough opponent, nerves dancing in her stomach like butterflies. But this time, when the referee called "play," Audrey took a deep breath, focused on the game, and trusted in the training she had committed to.

Point by point, she played with a joy that had been hidden beneath layers of worry. Even when she stumbled, she remembered her coach's words—each mistake was just a part of the journey. By the end of the match, whether she won or lost, the thrill of the game surged through her, illuminating the court with a newfound sparkle in her eyes. Audrey realized that she wasn't just playing badminton; she was learning about resilience, embracing challenges, and growing—the true spirit of an athlete.

BALANCING COMPETITION AND ENJOYMENT

Finding harmony between competition and enjoyment is difficult. The weight of performance expectations, particularly in a culture that venerates early specialization, can create a suffocating atmosphere. Concerns about burnout loom large, especially when young athletes are pushed to focus on a single sport, often driven by the relentless quest for success. Researchers have flagged this trend, warning that too much intensity can lead to fatigue and a sense of disillusionment (López et al., 2019).

Take Sabrina, for instance. She was once the shining star of the figure skating rink, infused with talent and the bright-eyed ambition of her parents, who envisioned her gliding elegantly through the Olympics. But as the hours on the ice piled up and the pressure mounted, that joy began to slip through her fingers like ice melting in the sun. The passion that had once fueled her spins and jumps faded away, overshadowed by a relentless focus on perfection.

Recognizing Sabrina's struggle, her coaches decided it was time for a refreshing change. They introduced a variety of activities, weaving in opportunities for creative expression and moments of playful competition. Suddenly, the rink felt less like a battleground and more like a canvas where she could paint her love for skating anew. With each session that focused on fun rather than flawless execution, Sabrina rediscovered the exhilaration that had captivated her heart all those years ago.

This transformation not only reignited her spirit but also served as a reminder to her parents. Achievement is valuable, no doubt, but joy—the thrill of being on the ice, of embracing the sport for what it offers beyond medals—holds a special place in the journey. Sabrina's story became one of balance, illustrating that the pursuit of excellence can coexist with the simple delight of just skating.

Developmental psychology provides an essential framework for understanding the multitude of factors influencing young athletes. By acknowledging the significance of age and development stages, nurturing supportive relationships, and balancing enjoyment with competition, we can create environments that support the well-rounded growth of young athletes. This foundation lays the groundwork for not just better athletes but well-rounded individuals, equipped to navigate both the challenges of sport and the complexities of life beyond the playing field.

THE PSYCHOLOGICAL DEVELOPMENT STAGES OF ATHLETES

The path of a young athlete winds through a landscape of grit and growth, where each sprint, each fallen tear, tells a story that extends far beyond the playing field. It's not just about mastering the perfect serve or achieving a personal best; it's about the metamorphosis that unfolds within. As children morph into teens and then mature into young adults, their minds and hearts expand, carving out a complex mosaic of cognitive, emotional, and social change shaped by their encounters in the world of sports. This chapter delves deep into those intricacies, illuminating the vital skills that emerge from their sporting journeys—skills that will serve them well beyond the confines of competition.

UNDERSTANDING COGNITIVE GROWTH

Cognitive development is an essential aspect of training for athletes, significantly shaping their ability to think critically and solve problems. Research supports the idea that participating in sports can markedly improve decision-making, strategic thinking, and judgment abilities (Helsen & Starkes, 1999). Whether on the track, field, or court, athletes are constantly faced with challenges that require quick thinking and effective strategies. Each game mirrors life's complexities, demanding not just physical ability but also a sharp mental acuity that develops through practice and experience. As they navigate these scenarios, athletes cultivate skills that transcend sports, equipping them for success in various aspects of their lives.

Take, for example, the journey of a young soccer player named Pearl. At just 12 years old, Pearl had already spent a few seasons on the field, mastering the art of dribbling and passing. But beyond the basic skills, she learned to visualize the game in a new way— understanding the dynamics of space and player positioning.

During a pivotal match, the tension was palpable, with the score tied and only minutes left on the clock. Pearl remembered her coach's words echoing in her mind: "Read the game." Trusting her instincts, she decided to shift her position, moving into open space just as one of her teammates was about to make a pass. In that split second, everything came together; she intercepted the ball perfectly and sent it flying toward the goal, leading her team to a triumphant score.

Such moments are more than just thrilling highlights of a match; they reflect the evolution of an athlete's cognitive skills shaped by experience and age. While younger players like Pearl often rely on their instincts and raw talent, it's the older athletes who start to bring in reflective practices, deepening their understanding of the game (Ericsson et al., 1993). Pearl's story illustrates how much there is to learn not just about the sport itself, but about thinking strategically when the pressure mounts, making the journey of an athlete not just one of physical growth, but of cognitive development as well.

The evolution of cognitive skills in athletes is not linear; instead, it is a balance between intrinsic motivation, environmental influences, training methodologies, and individual maturity. Coaches play a pivotal role in nurturing this development by creating training environments that encourage decision-making, foster critical thinking, and promote a deeper understanding of the game. By integrating cognitive challenges within their training regimens, coaches can help athletes like Pearl and others cultivate the mental acuity necessary to excel in competitive sports.

Cognitive development in athletes goes beyond the physical aspects of training, encompassing a broad spectrum of mental faculties crucial for success in sports. Through active engagement, experiential learning, and guided reflection, athletes progressively enhance their cognitive processes, leading to improved performance and a more profound appreciation of the complexities of their chosen sports. The stories of young athletes—like Pearl—serve as a testament to the vital role cognitive development plays in athletic achievement and personal growth.

EMOTIONAL REGULATION AND MATURITY

Emotional intelligence is a cornerstone of athletic success, particularly as young athletes navigate the rollercoaster of competition. Research shows that sports participation can foster emotional regulation and resilience (Gould & Udry, 1994). For many athletes, the ability to cope with stress, manage anxiety, handle failure, and celebrate success evolves continuously through their experiences.

Take the story of Luca, a high school swimmer, who faced a significant setback during his championship trials.

Emotional intelligence wasn't something Luca had ever given much thought to as he dove into the competition pool each season. Like most high school athletes, he was consumed by the thrill of the race, the adrenaline rush that came with the starting buzzer. But everything changed during his championship trials. As he stood at the edge of the pool, heart racing, and anticipation thick in the air, Luca's hopes took a nosedive. He didn't qualify for the finals, his performance faltering in ways he hadn't expected.

The disappointment crashed over him like a wave, dragging him down into a sea of self-doubt. It felt like the end of everything he had worked so hard for. But somewhere between the tears and the frustration, a flicker of resolve began to spark within him. He realized that wallowing in despair wouldn't rewrite his story. Instead, he sought guidance from his coach, who had always encouraged him to see challenges as opportunities.

"Let's break it down," Coach Emma said, her voice steady as they reviewed the race footage. As they analyzed each stroke and turn, Luca listened, absorbing the constructive feedback. The insights lit a new path forward, shifting his focus from his failures to the steps he could take to improve.

With each passing day, Luca began to practice emotional maturity, learning how to transform his initial frustration into a tactical game plan. The pool, once a source of anxiety, became a place for growth. He adopted visualization techniques, imagining himself gliding through the water with ease, and he embraced deep breathing exercises to quell the storm of nerves that often surged before a race.

Slowly but surely, as he applied these practices, everything started to change not just in the water, but in his heart and mind. Each practice session became a lesson not just in technique, but in resilience—the ability to bounce back from setbacks, to thrive under pressure. Luca found himself celebrating small victories, a refined stroke here, a quicker turn there, and with each improvement, his emotional strength deepened. The hardest races became building blocks, each one teaching him about not just swimming, but about the complexity of his own emotions.

By the time he arrived at the next championship trial, Luca had transformed. He stood at the pool's edge once more, but this time, he felt a sense of calm mixed with excited anticipation. No matter the outcome, he knew he was no longer just a swimmer; he was an athlete unafraid to embrace the emotional journey that defined his path.

IDENTITY FORMATION AND SELF-CONCEPT

Participation in sports plays a crucial role in the formation of identity for young athletes. Sports often become a significant part of their self-concept, influencing their self-esteem and self-worth. The pressure to conform to societal expectations around athletic success can be profound, requiring young athletes to navigate between personal aspirations and external validation (Brewer, 1993). For many, the thrill of crossing the finish line is more than a victory; it's a moment that defines them, cementing their self-esteem in the fragile ground of athletic success.

Steven was one of those athletes—gifted, determined, and unyieldingly driven. For him, each race was a chance to prove himself, to feel that rush of victory that sang in his veins and filled him with pride. The medals he collected became both his armor and his shackles. But when injuries took their toll and setbacks piled on, that same pressure felt like a vice, squeezing his sense of worth from every angle.

In the quiet moments away from the starting blocks, after the crowds had dispersed, he began to confront a deeper question: Who was he when the medals weren't around his neck? Through heartfelt talks with his coach and late-night conversations with his family, he slowly unraveled the tangled threads of his identity. They helped him realize that being a top runner didn't define him entirely, that his worth wasn't just tied to victory but also to the effort, resilience, and camaraderie he shared with his teammates.

This awakening didn't just ease the weight on his shoulders; it transformed how he approached the sport he loved. He learned to celebrate the effort he put in and to find joy in every stride, regardless of the outcome. As he shifted his focus from winning to nurturing sportsmanship and growth, the essence of his athletic experience blossomed into something richer and more fulfilling, illustrating that true identity comes not just with the trophies, but with the heart behind the pursuit.

MOTIVATION AND GOAL SETTING

Motivation plays a crucial role in keeping young athletes engaged in sports over the long haul. Many times, the difference lies in their sources of motivation: intrinsic versus extrinsic. Younger athletes tend to lean heavily on external validation, seeking praise and recognition from coaches and peers. In contrast, as athletes mature, they often develop a deeper, intrinsic love for their sport, finding joy in the challenges it presents and in the sheer act of playing. This shift is palpable, revealing not just a transition in skills and techniques, but a profound change in what sustains their passion for the game. This theme runs deep in the life of Iris, a high school gymnast whose evolution mirrors the struggle between those external rewards and a more profound, intrinsic passion.

Iris entered the world of gymnastics with stars in her eyes. She thrived on the applause that echoed in the gym, the way the judges' scores dictated her worth at that moment. But there was a turning point in her story, a quiet awakening that shifted her gaze inward. Under the watchful eye of her coach, she began to peel back the layers of expectation. They set realistic goals that delved beyond the surface of competition; they focused on improvement, on mastering the art of the sport she had come to love.

Slowly, she learned to appreciate the challenge of perfecting a difficult routine, the thrill of nailing a dismount that had once eluded her. With each small victory, she embraced—like finally executing a flawless back handspring—her motivation blossomed. Setbacks morphed into invaluable lessons, stepping stones on her path to growth rather than insurmountable failures.

As Iris transitioned from chasing medals to cherishing her development, a profound change took root. She flourished not just as an athlete, but as a young woman driven by her passion. The gym became a sanctuary, a space where the applause faded to the background, replaced by the satisfying rhythm of hard work, resilience, and the joy found in each graceful leap. In her journey, Iris discovered that true motivation lies not in the accolades, but in the unyielding love for what she does—a lesson she'd carry far beyond the sport.

MOTIVATION: WHAT DRIVES YOUNG ATHLETES?

DEFINING INTRINSIC VS. EXTRINSIC MOTIVATION

Motivation is the unmistakable pulse that keeps young athletes running—whether it's a grueling afternoon of soccer practice or the uncertainty before a big meet. It's what pushes them to lace up their shoes and hit the field when their friends are out playing video games, and it often defines their journey in the world of sports. To really understand this journey, it's essential for coaches, parents, and athletes to recognize the delicate balance between intrinsic and extrinsic motivation.

Intrinsic motivation is like a hidden spark igniting within. It's the pure desire to move, to create, to excel simply for the love of it. Picture Sarah, a spirited 12-year-old gymnast who dazzles everyone with her grace. As she approaches the mat, her heart races—not for the applause or the medals but for the thrill of the tumble and the exhilaration of conquering a challenging routine. Each time she vaults into the air, she feels as if she's defying gravity, relishing not just the success but the sheer joy of the performance itself. This internal drive fuels her commitment, helping her to push through the sweat and the occasional frustration, connecting her passion with perseverance and a deep-rooted love for her sport.

Extrinsic motivation often dances to the tune of outside influences—like awards, applause, or a parent's approving nod. Take Alex, for instance, a hopeful soccer player whose heart races not for the thrill of the game, but for the glimmer of trophies and the warmth of his parents' pride. With every swift kick of the ball, he's not just chasing victory; he's chasing validation. While those shiny trophies can spark an initial fire, they can leave a bittersweet aftertaste, casting a shadow over the joy of the game. Deci and Ryan's Self-Determination Theory reminds us that this kind of drive can sometimes fizzle out, leaving athletes like Alex caught in a cycle of seeking approval rather than finding true fulfillment in their passion.

THE ROLE OF PASSION IN PERFORMANCE

Intrinsic motivation nurtures a deeper passion for the sport, leading to heightened emotional engagement and improved performance over time. This passion can become a motivating force that encourages sustained effort and resilience, even in the face of setbacks. Young athletes who are intrinsically motivated, such as Caitlin, a 14-year-old track runner, often find themselves practicing long after the scheduled training session has ended, propelled by their love for running rather than the need for external validation.

Caitlin laced up her worn-out running shoes, the familiar scent of the track filling her senses. At just 14, she was a rising star in local track meets, but it wasn't the medals or the accolades that drew her to the sport. No, for Caitlin, it was something deeper—something that kept her on the track long after her teammates had packed up and gone home.

As the sun dipped below the horizon, painting the sky in hues of orange and pink, Caitlin lost herself in the rhythm of her feet pounding against the asphalt. Each stride was a release, each breath a testament to her passion for running. The pressure of competition faded away, replaced by the simple joy of movement. There was no coach watching her, no parents cheering from the sidelines—just her and the track, a place where she felt truly alive.

Her friends often marveled at her dedication. "Why do you practice so much? Don't you get tired?" they would ask, eyebrows raised in disbelief. Caitlin simply shrugged with a smile. "The more I run, the more I feel alive," she would say, her eyes sparkling with the thrill of the pursuit rather than any desire for recognition.

Research has shown that athletes like Caitlin, driven by a love for their sport rather than a craving for external approval, often achieve exceptional results. They pour their hearts into every practice, seeking feedback, refining their techniques, and reveling in the process of improvement. Caitlin was no exception; her intrinsic motivation fueled countless hours of practice, continuous learning, and an unfaltering resilience that saw her through the rough patches.

Indeed, Caitlin embodied the spirit of what it meant to be a true athlete. It wasn't just about winning; it was about embracing every moment on the track, every challenge along the way. And as she finished her last lap under the fading light, breathing heavily yet filled with a sense of peace, she knew this love for running was her guiding force—a passion that would carry her onward, regardless of the hurdles that lay ahead.

IMPACT OF EXTRINSIC REWARDS

Extrinsic rewards can seem like a magic wand, granting a burst of motivation when they shower praise and prizes. In the beginning, they shone brightly for Alycia, a spirited 15-year-old swimmer. The thrill of standing on the podium, gold medals glimmering under the bright lights, filled her with joy. Each race felt electric, her heart racing not just from the competition, but from the cheers and the anticipation of victory.

Yet, as the crowds grew larger and the expectations weighed heavier, the atmosphere shifted. The weight of everyone else's dreams began to press down on her, like a cold blanket stifling her spirit. It wasn't long before racing turned from exhilaration to anxiety. The simple joy of slicing through water felt like a chore; thoughts of what others expected replaced the thrill of competition. With every race, the pressure mounted, leading to shaky performances and, ultimately, a painful retreat from the sport she once adored.

This journey serves as a potent reminder of the paradox of external rewards. While they can elevate enthusiasm in the moment, they can just as easily drain the intrinsic joy from the experience. Research suggests that when extrinsic accolades overshadow the pure love of the craft, they risk stifling creativity and diminishing engagement. For Alycia, the thrill of being in the water was lost beneath layers of expectations and pressure.

It becomes clear that a balanced approach—one that embraces both the thrill of achievement and the joy of participation—could create a healthier space for young athletes. When the applause fades and the medals tarnish, what remains is the simple pleasure of swimming, a treasure worth nurturing far beyond the splash of victory.

CULTURAL AND SOCIAL INFLUENCES

Cultural expectations and peer dynamics contribute significantly to young athletes' motivation. In some communities, sporting success is highly valued, creating a competitive environment that can place intense pressure on young athletes like Emma, who feels the weight of family expectations to excel in volleyball. This societal pressure often overshadows the joy of participation, potentially leading to burnout or withdrawal from the sport altogether.

The gym buzzed with the sound of sneakers squeaking against polished wood, the air thick with the scent of sweat and determination. For Emma, each practice was a dance line, choreographed not only by her love for volleyball but also by the heavy expectations that trailed her every move. In her small town, athletic ability was a badge of honor worn with pride, often determining your place in the social hierarchy. Success on the court didn't just earn applause; it brought admiration, respect, and even love from her family.

But with that admiration came an unbearable weight. As Emma leaped for yet another spike, the echoes of her parents' voices danced in her head—"You have to win this game. You need to show them what you can do." Their hopes wrapped around her like vines, squeezing tighter with every match. What should have been a celebration of skill and teamwork often morphed into a gauntlet of expectations, where losing felt like a deeply personal failure.

The exhilaration of the game dimmed, overshadowed by the ever-present pressure to perform at her peak. Fun flickered in and out of her focus, replaced by a relentless drive to meet an ideal that seemed just out of reach. It was a treacherous path, and as Emma moved through practices, worn down day by day, she often found herself questioning—was it still worth it?

On the other hand, when positive peer influences and a nurturing community vibe collide, something magical happens: athletes find joy and a sense of belonging in their sports. It's not just about trophies or medals; it's about the thrill of the game and the shared laughter with teammates. Coaches and parents need to recognize these outside pressures and open up conversations about what success really means for each athlete. By encouraging them to chase personal joy instead of just societal approval, they can help reshape how young athletes view their journey in sports.

STRATEGIES TO FOSTER INTRINSIC MOTIVATION

Creating a space where intrinsic motivation can flourish is key to fostering lasting joy and commitment in sports. For coaches, parents, and athletes looking to cultivate this environment, here are some practical strategies to consider:

Encourage Self-Assessment: Help young athletes to reflect on their own performances, guiding them to measure their achievements against their own personal goals instead of comparing themselves to others.

Emphasize Mastery: Shift the focus to the journey of skill development, celebrating the small victories that come with mastering new techniques. This empowers athletes to take pride in their growth and progress.

Promote Autonomy: Engage athletes in the decision-making process regarding their training and competition schedules, fostering a sense of ownership and responsibility for their athletic journey.

Create a Supportive Environment: Build a culture where teamwork and camaraderie thrive, replacing a cutthroat atmosphere with one that values cooperation and mutual support.

Cultivate Enjoyment: Organize activities that highlight the joy of participating in sports, such as fun game-day celebrations or relaxed practice sessions that foster friendships among teammates.

Recognize Effort and Progress: Celebrate the dedication and improvements of each athlete, focusing on their hard work and the joy of playing, rather than solely on wins and losses.

By embracing these approaches, young athletes can cultivate a deep-seated motivation that transforms the way they experience their sport. As they delve into the sheer joy of what they do, they find themselves not just participating, but truly living for the game. This newfound passion often grows into a lasting commitment to physical activity, building the resilience needed to overcome any challenges that arise. In the end, it's about more than just winning; it's about cherishing the journey and the lessons learned along the path.

Grasping the nuances of motivation—especially the fine balance between intrinsic desires and external rewards—can transform young athletes' journeys into something remarkable. It's not merely about the trophies or accolades; it's about the thrill of the game, the joy in the sweat, and the friendships forged in the heat of competition. As they navigate the ups and downs, understanding what fuels their passion and drive will not only elevate their performance but also deepen their love for their sport, ensuring that the memories they create are as cherished as the goals they score.

THE ROLE OF SELF-EFFICACY IN ATHLETIC SUCCESS

DEFINITION AND ORIGINS OF SELF-EFFICACY

The concept of self-efficacy originates from the work of psychologist Albert Bandura, who introduced this term as part of his broader theory of social cognitive theory in the 1970s. Self-efficacy is defined as an individual's belief in their capabilities to perform specific tasks and to overcome challenges in various situations (Bandura, 1977). This belief plays a fundamental role in how individuals approach goals, tasks, and challenges, particularly in the realm of sports.

For young athletes, the perception of their ability to succeed significantly influences their motivation, persistence, and ultimately their success. Bandura emphasized that self-efficacy is context-specific; an athlete may feel confident in their ability to run a marathon but lack the same belief in their ability to compete in a sprint. This specificity allows coaches and athletes to focus on developing self-efficacy in particular areas, tailoring training and support to enhance performance across different skills and disciplines.

IMPACT ON PERFORMANCE

Extensive research has demonstrated a direct correlation between self-efficacy and athletic performance. High self-efficacy levels are associated with improved performance metrics in young athletes across various sports disciplines, from swimming to soccer. For example, a meta-analysis by Moritz et al. (2000) showed that self-efficacy is a robust predictor of performance outcomes, presenting implications for motivation and persistence.

Eva stood at the edge of the pool, the air thick with chlorine and anticipation. At sixteen, she was no stranger to the competitive swim circuit, but sprint events always seemed to slip through her fingers like water itself. Each competition loomed like an unscalable wall, her heart racing not with excitement but with the weight of expectations—hers and those from countless coaches, parents, and peers.

But this year felt different. Working closely with Coach Bill, she had embarked on a journey beyond mere technique—one that ventured deep into the realm of mindset. They had dissected each race, pinpointing the moments when doubt crept in and derailed her focus. Together, they crafted a roadmap filled with small, achievable goals, each one a step toward a larger prize. It was in these little victories—perfecting her dive, mastering her flip turn, even shaving off tenths of a second in practice—that Eva found glimpses of confidence.

It wasn't just training; it was a shift in how she viewed herself as an athlete. That transformation simmered beneath the surface until it finally erupted during her next competition. Standing on the block, heart pounding and nerves buzzing, she recalled the countless hours spent honing her skills, the supportive words from Coach Bill ringing in her ears. "You own this, Eva. Trust your training."

When the starting gun fired, something clicked. With every stroke, she felt her doubts dissipate, replaced by an exhilarating rush of empowerment. It was like gliding through water, not fighting against it. As she touched the wall and turned to look at the clock, disbelief flooded her senses—a five-second improvement. The moment was electrifying, a testament to the undeniable link between her budding self-efficacy and newfound performance.

Eva's story was not just about swimming; it was about the powerful message lurking beneath the surface. With each small victory, she had stitched together a tapestry of belief, crafting an athlete who embraced challenges rather than shying away from them. It was a reminder that the mind could be as formidable an opponent as any rival in the lanes beside her, and sometimes, all it took was a little faith in oneself to transform potential into reality.

SELF-EFFICACY VS. SELF-ESTEEM

While self-efficacy and self-esteem may sound similar, they are distinctly different constructs. Self-esteem refers to an individual's overall sense of self-worth, whereas self-efficacy pertains specifically to one's belief in their ability to succeed in particular tasks or challenges. This distinction is vital for coaches and young athletes. For example, an athlete may feel valued and confident in general, but if they doubt their ability to execute specific skills, they may struggle to perform well under pressure. Simply encouraging young athletes to possess high self-esteem may not address the underlying beliefs that impact their performance.

Christian, a 15-year-old soccer player with dreams as bright as the stadium lights, stood on the edge of the field, heart pounding like a drum. With every passing match, the cheers of his family and friends echoed in his ears, filling him with pride. But when the whistle blew and the stakes were high, a shroud of pressure wrapped around him, stifling his confidence. Despite his knack for weaving through defenders and scoring goals in practice, the thought of taking a game-winning penalty kick left him frozen, his self-assurance crumbling at the most critical moments.

Determined to conquer his fears, Christian embarked on a journey that would redefine his approach to the game. He committed to targeted drills, practicing shot after shot until the movement felt like second nature. The field became his sanctuary, where he could let the ball dance at his feet, and in each sweat-drenched session, he built a foundation of skills designed for moments of triumph.

But practice alone wouldn't do—the pressure needed to be tangible. With the help of his coach, he faced the challenge head-on, simulating real game scenarios. The noise of the crowd, the ticking clock, the weight of expectation—they all became familiar friends, forcing Christian to confront the anxiety that had clung to him like a stubborn shadow.

Days turned into weeks, and slowly, the transformation took root. With each successful kick during practice, his belief in himself solidified, blooming into a newfound confidence that radiated on the field. By the time he faced his first true test in a closely contested match, it was as if he had stepped onto that pitch with a different heart—a heart unshackled by old fears.

When the moment finally arrived—a penalty kick with the game on the line—Christian inhaled deeply, the world around him fading into the background. He visualized the goal, the ball gliding smoothly into the back corner, and as he took his shot, he felt the exhilaration of his hard work coursing through him. The net rippled in response, a victorious dance that confirmed what he had always hoped: the journey from self-doubt to self-efficacy was no longer just a dream, but his reality. The cheers that erupted from the stands rang sweeter than ever, a testament to the fortitude within him.

BUILDING SELF-EFFICACY THROUGH MASTERY EXPERIENCES

The journey toward mastery unfolds like a carefully charted course. These youthful competitors need more than just talent on the field; they require opportunities to tackle tasks that they can steadily conquer. Just as a budding musician learns to play one note at a time before mastering a symphony, athletes thrive when they can set achievable goals and steadily navigate through increasingly challenging hurdles.

As they work diligently to meet each goal, their confidence blossoms, nurtured by the success of each small victory. Research, including the insights of Bandura (1997), underscores this idea: the experiences where athletes triumph and fulfill their ambitions become the bedrock of their self-efficacy, instilling within them a sense of belief that propels them forward. In this dynamic dance of effort and achievement, young athletes not only sharpen their skills but also fortify their inner resolve, preparing them for the competitions that lie ahead.

At twelve years old, Lana stood at the edge of the softball field, the sun casting a warm glow on her determined face. Every day after school, she dedicated herself to a training routine crafted by her coach, who understood that mastery wasn't a single leap but a series of careful, measured steps.

The journey began with simple drills: throwing, catching, and basic swings. Lana felt the thrill of success wash over her every time she nailed a simple catch or hit a ball just right. Each small victory transformed into fuel, igniting her belief in what she could achieve.

As the weeks passed, the challenges grew more complex. Drills that once made her stomach flutter with nerves became second nature. With every step up the ladder, her confidence soared, like a ball crackling through the air. She was no longer just another player; she was a competitor, thriving in the rhythm of the game.

Then came the regional championship, a culmination of her hard work and a test of her skills. As she stood at the plate, bat in hand, memories of countless practices flashed in her mind. The weight of expectations mixed with the exhilaration of the moment, yet she felt ready.

When she swung, the crack of the bat echoed like a triumphant cheer. With her heart pounding in her chest, Lana's confidence transformed into raw power, propelling her team to victory. In that moment, she didn't just win a game; she proved to herself that with determination and the right guidance, even the highest peaks could be scaled.

THE ROLE OF POSITIVE FEEDBACK AND SOCIAL SUPPORT

Encouragement from coaches, peers, and family is crucial for enhancing self-efficacy in young athletes. Social support can provide the emotional backing necessary to bolster belief in one's abilities. Research emphasizes that positive feedback not only increases motivation but also enhances the athlete's self-perception of competence (Smith et al., 2017).

In the world of young athletes, the voices of coaches, teammates, and family members often play a vital role in shaping who they become on and off the field. It's not just about running faster or jumping higher; it's about the heart behind those actions. The right words at the right moment can light a fire inside a young athlete, boosting their belief in what they're capable of achieving.

Twelve-year-old Connor lived for basketball. With each bounce of his worn-out sneakers against the gym floor, he felt a surge of excitement, but that thrill was often overshadowed by the gnawing doubt that crept in just as quickly. On the surface, he seemed like any other kid with a love for the game, but beneath it all, his confidence floundered like a ship in turbulent waters.

Coach Thompson saw it, the way Connor hesitated when it was time to shoot or the way his shoulders slumped after a missed layup. Instead of criticism, Coach took a different route. He pulled Connor aside after practice, his voice steady and encouraging. "You've improved your free throws significantly, Connor. That last session, I could see how hard you were working on your form." Each word was a lifeline, thrown at just the right moment.

At home, Connor could always count on the cheer of his family. His younger sister waved a homemade sign from the bleachers, his parents shouted his name like he was the star of the show. This support wrapped around him, tangible and warm, helping him reshape the narrative in his mind. He remembered their smiles every time he stepped onto the court, drawing courage from their belief in him.

As the weeks turned into months, the timid boy began to transform. He started to take those bold, heady risks—going for shots he would have previously shied away from, charging down the court in pursuit of a layup, and even calling for the ball when the game was on the line. With each successful shot, his confidence bloomed, until the whispers of doubt faded into the background.

And then came the moment that would define his season: the championship game. The score was tied, seconds felt like hours, and the gym was filled with the thunderous pulse of anticipation. Connor, standing at the free-throw line, paused to breathe, the whole world shrinking into that one shot. He remembered Coach's words and the love of his family, and with a deep breath, he released the ball. The satisfying swish that followed echoed in his ears, marking the shift from boy to athlete in a single heartbeat. He was no longer just Connor, the kid who played basketball; he was Connor, the kid who could make clutch free throws when it mattered most.

EFFECTS OF VICARIOUS EXPERIENCES

Observational learning, or vicarious experiences, also plays a pivotal role in shaping self-efficacy. Young athletes who watch their role models—such as successful peers or professional athletes—can be inspired to aspire to greater achievements and adopt similar behaviors. Research indicates that witnessing others achieve success can significantly enhance an observer's self-efficacy (Bandura, 1986).

Valeria was like any other 13-year-old, her heart racing with dreams that seemed just out of reach. She was a track athlete, vibrant and determined, with a passion for running that blurred the lines between reality and aspiration. One crisp Saturday morning, she stood in the bleachers, feeling the chill of early spring in her bones as she watched her idol—an inspiring local Olympic runner—take her mark.

The whistle blew, and in that moment, time felt suspended. Valeria leaned forward, eyes glued to the track, as the runner took off like a bullet, her strides long and smooth, a perfect dance of speed and grace. When the race ended, the cheers rose like a tidal wave, and Valeria felt a rush she couldn't quite describe. The runner had achieved a personal best, and the glow of achievement radiated from her, as if it were lighting the path for Valeria to follow.

Fueled by that electric moment, Valeria returned to her training regimen with renewed energy. She pored over a personalized training program, marked up the days on her calendar, and filled her water bottle with the fervor of someone on a quest. Each lap she completed was a testament to the belief that had sparked within her that day at the meet.

Weeks turned into months, and with each heartbeat pushing her forward, Valeria found herself catching glimpses of her own potential. Then came the day of the big race. The familiar nerves twisted in her stomach, but this time, they were tinged with something new confidence. As the starting gun fired, Valeria launched herself down the track, the wind whipping past her, echoing the rhythm of her heartbeat.

When she crossed the finish line, breathless and elated, she glanced at the clock. A full ten seconds had vanished from her previous best time. In that moment, Valeria realized the power of her vicarious journey—the belief that had bloomed from witnessing greatness, now rippling through her own veins, propelling her into a future bright with possibility.

SELF-EFFICACY IN OVERCOMING ADVERSITY

Perhaps one of the most critical roles of self-efficacy is its influence on resilience—an athlete's ability to cope with setbacks, injuries, and failures. When young athletes possess a strong belief in their abilities, they are more likely to persist in the face of challenges. Studies have shown that a higher sense of self-efficacy fosters resilience and enables individuals to bounce back from adversity (Schunk, 2003).

Julian had always been a force on the wrestling mat, a promising young talent with dreams of championship glory. But as the season approached, everything came crashing down. A sudden injury—one that felt too harsh and too cruel—left him shattered, grappling not just with physical pain but with an overwhelming tide of doubt.

In the quiet moments following the diagnosis, Julian felt lost, the prospect of competition slipping through his fingers like grains of sand. But it was in those moments of vulnerability that the power of camaraderie began to weave its way back into his life. His coach, a steady figure who had seen countless victories and defeats, stepped in first. The coach's words were firm yet gentle, a reminder of the countless hours of sweat and determination Julian had already poured into his craft.

"Remember how far you've come," he said, his voice steady. "The work you've put in doesn't just disappear because of this setback. You've got the spirit of a champion."

His teammates rallied around him, a chorus of encouragement that filled the empty spaces left by his injury. They recalled the countless practices where they'd pushed each other to the brink, the bonds forged in sweat and struggle. They reminded him that this journey was never just about the trophies; it was about the grit, the grind, and the unwavering belief in oneself, even when all seemed lost.

With each physical therapy session, as he fought to reclaim his strength, Julian felt that support lifting him, shifting his mindset. The process was grueling, and some days were darker than others, but each small victory—lifting a little heavier, moving a little faster—rekindled a flicker of hope within him. Self-efficacy, he learned, was not just a concept; it was a living, breathing force that propelled him forward.

As championship day drew near, Julian stepped onto the mat not just as a competitor but as a testament to resilience. The roar of the crowd seemed to urge him on, a symphony of shared passion and belief. When the final whistle blew and he emerged victorious, it wasn't just a win on the scoreboard; it was a realization of what one could achieve in the face of adversity, a powerful reminder that resilience and self-belief could rewrite any story.

Julian understood that championships are not merely won on the mat; they begin in the heart, where the echoes of support and perseverance resonate, crafting the narratives that shape us long after the final match is over.

In the world of young athletes, self-efficacy stands as a cornerstone for success. It's not just about winning games or breaking records; it's about the belief in one's own abilities. When young athletes experience mastery—those moments when they nail a complicated move or score the game-winning goal—they build a confidence that creates a ripple effect in their performances.

Positive feedback from coaches and parents fuels this sense of accomplishment, turning small wins into a powerful sense of self-belief. Observational learning plays a crucial role too—seeing a teammate triumph can ignite a spark of possibility in a young athlete's mind. And when they face challenges, it's the resilience that comes from believing they can overcome obstacles that sets them apart.

Understanding how critical self-efficacy is lets coaches and parents take a more active role in nurturing it. When they support and encourage young athletes, they do more than prepare them for the next game; they empower them to thrive in all aspects of life. Through this lens, the journey of becoming an athlete transforms into a journey of growth and self-discovery, where every challenge becomes an opportunity, and every setback is a chance to rise again.

BUILDING RESILIENCE: OVERCOMING CHALLENGES IN SPORT

UNDERSTANDING RESILIENCE

Resilience isn't just a trait; it's a necessity for anyone who steps into the arena of competitive sports. It's the ability to rise from the ashes after a hard-fought defeat, to find strength in the face of injuries, and to transform an off-day into a stepping stone for tomorrow. In this high-stakes world, setbacks are more than just obstacles—they're lessons masked in disappointment, opportunities dressed in challenges.

Think of the athlete who stumbles on the track, takes a tumble, and feels the weight of the world crush their spirit. For some, that's a point of no return. But for resilient athletes, it's a moment to rise, assess, and adapt. Studies show that those who possess this resilience are often better equipped to navigate the emotional tempest that competition brings. They learn to perform amid the chaos of expectations and pressures, often achieving peak performance even when anxiety hangs heavy in the air (Gould & Udry, 1994).

These resilient competitors are the ones who bounce back, not just in their sport but in their mental well-being. They find joy in the grind, satisfaction in the struggle, and an undeniable drive that propels them forward. Resilience, then, is not merely an attribute; it's the backbone of an athlete's journey, a crucial ingredient in the recipe for success both on and off the field. It reminds us that while the journey may be fraught with challenges, it is also rich with the potential for growth, deeper connection, and ultimately, triumph.

MINDSET MASTERY

A crucial element of resilience is having a growth mindset—the belief that one's abilities can be developed through dedication and hard work (Dweck, 2006). This perspective fosters a love for learning and a resilience that is essential for great accomplishments. A key part of resilience lies in embracing a growth mindset —the idea that with effort and commitment, we can enhance our own abilities. This belief doesn't just promote a passion for learning; it cultivates the kind of resilience that paves the way for achieving remarkable things.

Ella stepped off the mat, her heart racing, but not from the thrill of competition. The loud clamor of applause faded into a hollow echo, drowned out by the weight of her thoughts. She had trained tirelessly for this moment, her body a vessel of sweat and dedication, yet the score flashed on the screen felt like a jab to her gut— far lower than she had hoped.

Disappointment soured the taste of victory she had long dreamed of. For a moment, all she could see were the missed opportunities, the stumbles in her routine that now felt magnified under the harsh fluorescent lights of the gymnasium. She blinked back tears, feeling the pinprick of failure piercing through her resolve.

But then there was Coach Marissa, with her steady presence that always seemed to cut through the noise. "Ella," she said, her voice calm yet firm, "let's not throw away this moment. Every setback is just an invitation to learn."

Instead of seeing her score as a verdict on her worth, Ella began to unravel the disappointment thread by thread. Coach Marissa helped her dissect her performance, pointing out not just what went wrong, but highlighting the small victories—how her leaps had improved, or how her landing was nearly flawless. Slowly, Ella learned to embrace her missteps as growth opportunities rather than as evidence of her inadequacy.

With every practice, she shifted her focus. It wasn't about the score anymore; it was about progress and passion. She poured her energy into perfecting her skills, her routines gradually transforming into a dance of strength and grace. Over the months, each drop in score became a stepping stone, guiding her toward improvement rather than pulling her down into despair.

And then, one day, as the season unfolded, she stepped onto the mat again, a slight tremor of anticipation coursing through her. With every move, she felt the culmination of hard work and determination: the sweat, the late nights, and the reframed mindset all colliding into something beautiful. When the scores were announced, a rush of elation surged through her; she had earned her place among the top gymnasts in her region.

In that moment, as the crowd erupted into applause, Ella understood the true essence of her journey. Setbacks weren't symbols of failure but rather powerful motivators that shaped her path to success. With every hurdle she faced, she learned that resilience could transform vulnerability into strength. The gymnast who once faltered in the face of pressure stood tall now, a testament to the transformative power of a growth mindset.

TECHNIQUES FOR SHIFTING PERSPECTIVE

Reflection Journals: Athletes can embrace the power of journaling to chronicle their journeys, capturing the highs and lows of their experiences. By noting what worked, what fell short, and the insights gleaned along the way, they cultivate a practice of self-reflection. This ongoing dialogue with themselves isn't just about recording events; it's a tool that nurtures resilience, helping them navigate the ever-changing landscape of sports and life itself.

Positive Reframing: By guiding athletes to recognize and express a positive spin on their setbacks, we can transform their viewpoint and bolster their resilience.

COPING MECHANISMS

In the world of young athletes, the pressure can sometimes feel like an overwhelming weight, pressing down with every practice, every competition, and every assignment due. It's a reality they know all too well—a race against time to balance their dreams with the demands of life. But as they navigate this tumultuous journey, finding ways to cope becomes essential to their resilience.

Take Sebastian, for instance. An ambitious soccer player, he often found himself paralyzed by the fear of missing the mark during games. It felt insurmountable until he stumbled upon mindfulness —a simple practice that transformed everything. During grueling training sessions, he began focusing on deep-breathing exercises and paying attention to the rhythm of his body as he moved. Suddenly, the noise of expectations quieted, and he discovered an anchor within himself. That calmness on the field translated into sharper moves, and, with it, the realization that he could master the game—not just physically, but mentally as well.

Then there's Lyla, a dedicated swimmer with speed in her veins. Races were always accompanied by a storm of nerves, but she learned to harness that energy through visualization. Closer to the big day, she would close her eyes and play a mental movie of her race—every stroke, every turn crafted perfectly in her mind. As she imagined slicing through the water, she felt the confidence she needed. When the starting gun went off, instead of succumbing to anxiety, she already knew how to dance through the water, earning her a personal best that day.

And let's not forget about self-talk. Young athletes often grapple with their inner critics, voices that insist they aren't enough. Yet, through practice, they can turn that script around. Instead of drowning in doubts of "I can't do this," they learn to affirm themselves with a resolute "I will give my best effort." This simple shift in perspective can be a game-changer, transforming setbacks into mile stones.

In the hearts of young athletes lies incredible potential, and by cultivating coping strategies like mindfulness, visualization, and positive self-talk, they'll find that resilience isn't just about enduring—it's about thriving in the pursuit of their passions.

BUILDING SUPPORT NETWORKS

Young athletes do not have to navigate pressures and setbacks alone. The weight of expectations can feel heavy, like a thick fog settling on their shoulders. But they don't have to face that fog alone. Finding a robust support network is key to cultivating resilience in the face of setbacks. Coaches offer guidance, teammates provide camaraderie, families supply unconditional love, and mental health professionals lend their expertise. Each connection adds a layer of strength to the athlete's journey, illuminating the path forward when challenges arise. In this intricate dance of support, young athletes learn to rise, not just as competitors, but as individuals who can weather the storms together.

Valentina laced up her worn running shoes, the familiar scent of the track mingling with the crisp autumn air. But today, that scent felt heavy, weighed down by the echoes of her recent defeats. It wasn't just the losses that gnawed at her; it was the creeping self-doubt, a relentless whisper that questioned her worth as an athlete. With each race that slipped through her fingers, her confidence frayed a little more.

Coach Sanchez noticed Valentina's struggle. He called the team together, and instead of falling into the usual routines, he invited them to speak openly. "Let's share where we feel stuck," he said, his voice steady, encouraging. At first, the silence was thick, filled with unspoken fears. But as Valentina opened up about her insecurities, a wave of relief washed over her.

One by one, her teammates followed, sharing their own experiences of failure and fear. In that moment, they weren't just individuals; they were a collective, bound by the acknowledgment of their struggles. Valentina found herself nodding as she listened to their stories, her heart swelling with a newfound sense of belonging. Each loss morphed into a shared learning experience, something they could all grow from together.

As the season unfolded, the team's supportive dialogue fostered resilience. Valentina learned to embrace her setbacks, not as markers of defeat but as stepping stones toward improvement. They trained harder, cheered louder, and held each other accountable. The spirit of unity transformed what could have been a fading season into a series of triumphs.

By the time the final race approached, Valentina felt different. It wasn't just about winning; it was about running alongside her friends, sharing the journey, and celebrating their growth. As she crossed the finish line, the roar of her teammates enveloped her, reminding her that she was never alone in her struggles. Together, they had built something far more valuable than trophies: a team grounded in triumphs, trials, and unwavering support.

LEARNING FROM FAILURE

Failure weaves itself into the fabric of every athlete's journey, often revealing truths that success cannot. The story of Michael Jordan stands as a testament to this reality. He didn't make his high school basketball team on his first try—an experience that could have crushed his spirit. Instead, it lit a fire within him, compelling him to hone his craft relentlessly. His determination transformed that initial setback into strength, catapulting him to become one of the greatest basketball players to ever grace the court.

In a small town, a group of gymnasts at a local academy found themselves in a similar predicament. Despite months of grueling practice and sacrifice, they failed to qualify for the state championships. At first, it felt like the end of the road, a harsh reality that left them disheartened.

But as they gathered for their weekly practice, an air of resilience began to take shape among them. Instead of shying away from their disappointment, they leaned into it, discussing the areas where they faltered. They shared their frustrations and fears, turning their individual weaknesses into collective goals. Each gymnast emerged with a renewed sense of purpose, viewing their failure not as a dead end, but as an opportunity to grow.

With every tumble and twist, they transformed their setbacks into lessons, emerging stronger and more unified as a team. Their journey continued, and when the next season dawned, their performances spoke of perseverance, grit, and an unwavering belief in themselves—qualities that transcended the routines they executed on the mat. These young athletes were learning that failure is not a mark of the end but merely a part of the landscape of success.

CREATING A RESILIENCE TRAINING PLAN

To truly build resilience in athletes, coaches need to take a personalized approach that blends mental and emotional strategies with physical recovery methods. Imagine a young runner named Claire, who's been struggling with anxiety before races. By implementing a tailored resilience training plan, she can turn her challenges into stepping stones toward improvement.

Assessment: First, Claire sits down with her coach, who gently probes into her past experiences. What tough moments did she face on the track? Did she freeze up before a big race? Together, they identify her strengths—like her tenacity—and pinpoint areas where she can grow, such as her anxious thoughts.

Skill Development: Next, they dive into resilience skills. With her coach's guidance, Claire learns the art of mindfulness meditation, allowing her to find calm amidst the storm of competition. They practice visualization, where she imagines herself gliding across the finish line, buoyed by confidence. They create a mantra that Claire can repeat to herself, shifting her inner dialogue from fear to strength.

Physical Recovery: Just as vital as her mental training, they emphasize the importance of physical recovery. Claire adopts new habits: she crafts a nutrition plan filled with energy-giving foods and embraces rest days as sacred. The coach introduces her to rehabilitation exercises that not only heal her body but also bolster her mental resilience, showing her that recovery is part of the journey—an essential tool for overcoming both physical and emotional hurdles.

Support Systems: Throughout this process, Claire learns the value of reaching out. She and her coach establish a regular check-in schedule, but Claire also starts confiding in her teammates and a trusted mental health professional. This support network becomes her safety net, reminding her she doesn't have to navigate everything alone.

Routine Evaluation: Finally, they schedule regular evaluations. At each checkpoint, Claire reflects on her progress and the growth she's experienced. Have her coping mechanisms shifted? Is she feeling less anxious on race days? They adjust the plan as needed, ensuring it evolves alongside her development.

In this nurturing environment, Claire begins to transform challenges into opportunities, developing a resilience that prepares her not just for races, but for life's vast array of obstacles.

Building resilience isn't just about weathering storms; it's about turning those storms into the wind beneath your wings. For young athletes, learning to be resilient can do wonders—it sharpens performance, nurtures mental health, and equips them for the rollercoaster of competition. Embracing a growth mindset paves the way for seeing setbacks as opportunities, while effective coping strategies become crucial tools in their kit. Surrounding themselves with a supportive network of friends, family, and coaches creates a safety net during tough times. Every stumble is a lesson, every misstep a chance to grow. By crafting a resilience training plan tailored just for them, these young competitors can cultivate the mental strength they need to excel not only in sports but also in the game of life.

STRESS MANAGEMENT TECHNIQUES FOR YOUNG

UNDERSTANDING STRESSORS IN SPORTS

Young athletes often find themselves facing unique challenges that can create significant stress. Performance expectations arise not just from personal aspirations but also from coaches, peers, parents, and the larger sporting community. For instance, 14-year-old Sophie, an aspiring gymnast, felt intense pressure to secure a place in her region's elite training program. With her peers scoring in the 9.5 range on vault routines, Sophie started to compare herself unfavorably, causing her stress levels to soar (Smith, 2020).

Fourteen-year-old Sophie had always felt at home on the gym mat, flipping through the air with an elegance that made her heart race. But lately, the joy had begun to fade, overshadowed by the weight of expectation. As the regional elite training program approached, Sophie found herself waking up in the middle of the night, her mind racing with scores and comparisons.

Her friends—fierce and talented gymnasts—were not just competing; they were soaring, consistently hitting 9.5s in their vault routines, their smiles radiant with triumph. Each time Sophie watched them practice, her own self-doubt crept in like a relentless shadow. The thrill of competition felt more like a shackle, wrapping tightly around her heart, squeezing until she could hardly breathe.

"What if I'm not good enough?" she whispered to herself, the question echoing long after the last notes of the gym's upbeat music faded. The idea of failure loomed large, and as the weight of her aspirations pressed down, Sophie could feel the ground beneath her feet crumbling ever so slightly.

Competition pressure, particularly during high-stakes events, can exacerbate anxiety. Samuel, a talented young swimmer, experienced panic attacks before competitions due to the overwhelming expectation of winning. This not only hindered his performance but took a toll on his enthusiasm for the sport (Jones et al., 2021). Peer comparisons heighten these stressors, particularly in team sports, where young athletes may feel they need to outperform their friends or maintain a certain status within the team.

In the world of competitive swimming, the shimmering water is both a sanctuary and a source of torment for young athletes like Samuel. He once entered the pool with a carefree heart, his strokes slicing through the water like a knife. But as the stakes grew higher, that joy began to slip away, replaced by an all-consuming dread. The night before each big event, panic wrapped around him like a heavy cloak, suffocating his spirit as thoughts of expectations swirled in his mind.

Samuel's talent was undeniable—he was the kind of swimmer whose presence could light up the room at practice with laughter and camaraderie. Yet, the weight of his own ambition loomed large, and the pressure to excel became a relentless shadow. He saw his teammates' successes as benchmarks he needed to beat, friends who once buoyed his spirits now contributing to a tide that threatened to pull him under. Instead of feeling uplifted by their accomplishments, he felt trapped in a race with invisible blades, each lap turning into a reminder of what he feared he might lose: his joy for the sport, his sense of self, and the untainted love he once had for the water.

As Samuel faced the starting block, he realized that the joy of swimming was being drowned out by the very expectations that should have inspired him, leaving him gasping for freedom in a pool that had become both familiar and frightening.

The research underscores that these pressures can take a significant toll on both mental health and athletic performance. A study by Gould et al. (2019) reveals a concerning trend: young athletes grappling with performance anxiety are at a heightened risk of burnout, and many ultimately choose to step away from the sports they once loved. To combat these challenges, it's vital that young athletes adopt robust stress management strategies, fostering the mental resilience they need to thrive both on and off the field.

RECOGNIZING PHYSICAL AND EMOTIONAL SYMPTOMS

Understanding the physiological and emotional signs of stress is crucial for athletes to develop self-awareness. Common symptoms of performance anxiety include an increased heart rate, irritability, difficulty concentrating, and fatigue. For example, 15-year-old Erik, a soccer forward, noticed that he would become easily frustrated with himself during practice when he couldn't focus on the game plan. His chronic fatigue led him to dread training sessions rather than look forward to them, ultimately affecting his performance during matches (Davis & Hollander, 2020).

In the heart of a bustling practice field, 15-year-old Erik felt a familiar knot tightening in his stomach. He had always loved soccer—the exhilaration of the game, the rush of scoring a goal— but lately, the joy seemed to slip through his fingers like sand. As a forward, he should have been charging ahead, but instead, he found himself mired in frustration. Every whistle sounded like a judgment, and every missed pass felt like a personal failure.

His heart raced, pounding against his chest as if trying to escape the clutches of performance anxiety. The vibrant chatter of his teammates faded into the background, replaced by the nagging thoughts that crowded his mind. Why couldn't he focus? Why was he, usually so quick on his feet, suddenly clumsy and weary?

Erik knew he was tired—bone-deep tired. It wasn't just physical fatigue; it was emotional exhaustion that made him dread each training session rather than anticipate the thrill of the game. The fun felt lost, replaced by the weight of expectations that had begun to feel suffocating.

But in moments of desperation, he remembered his coach's advice: "Notice the signs, Erik. Understanding what you're feeling is half the battle." With that thought, he made a quiet promise to himself. He decided to take a step back, to learn about the signals his body was sending—the rattling heart, the growing irritability, the fog that clouded his concentration.

As the sun dipped below the horizon and the practice ended, Erik opened his notebook—a simple, unassuming journal filled with half-formed thoughts and scraps of ideas. He started to write, pouring his feelings onto the page: frustration, fear, fatigue. With each line, he felt a little lighter, the weight of his worries lifting just enough to breathe.

He also began practicing mindfulness—taking a moment to breathe in deeply, to feel the ground beneath his feet, to hear the world around him without judgment. And on particularly tough days, he sought out Coach Mia, someone he trusted implicitly, and together they talked through his challenges, exploring ways to manage the storm brewing within.

In understanding himself, Erik slowly transformed his struggle into a new game plan—one that focused not only on his physical prowess but also on his emotional resilience. He could feel a shift, a budding sense of control over his own mental landscape, and for the first time in a long time, he could see the glimmer of hope on the horizon. It wouldn't be easy, but with each step toward self-awareness, he was charting a path not just to improved performance, but to rediscovering the joy of the game he once loved so much.

Recognizing these signs enables athletes to take proactive steps toward managing their emotional states. Developing an understanding of their own bodies and emotions gives athletes the tools to implement coping strategies before stress escalates. By journaling feelings, practicing mindfulness, or discussing experiences with a trusted coach or friend, young athletes can begin to articulate their challenges, paving the way for healthier coping mechanisms.

GOAL SETTING FOR FOCUS AND MOTIVATION

Setting realistic, measurable, and achievable goals can help ease stress by bringing clarity and focus to our lives. Take, for example, a basketball player who dreams of glory on the court. Instead of fixating on the unattainable goal of winning every single game, they might choose to focus on a more tangible target—raising their free throw percentage by just 10%. This shift in mindset not only cultivates a healthier motivation but also lightens the burden of perfectionism, allowing them to play with more enjoyment and less anxiety.

In the dizzying whirl of competition, Andy often felt the weight of expectations pressing down on him, a tightness in his chest that made each match harder to face. The roar of the crowd, the piercing whistle of the referee, and the palpable tension in the air seemed to amplify the pressure he felt, turning what should be an exhilarating experience into a source of anxiety. He wasn't alone; a study by Eklund et al. in 2021 found that many young athletes shared this burden, trapped in a cycle of performance anxiety that overshadowed their love for the sport.

Yet, amid the pressure, a light flickered for him when he made a pivotal decision to shift his focus from outcomes to practice goals. Instead of fixating on winning or losing, the relentless pursuit of trophies and accolades, he set his sights on mastering a particular move—from perfecting his footwork to refining his technique with a specific skill. This small yet significant change transformed his perception of training. Each session became an opportunity for growth rather than a countdown to judgment. With every small success, whether it was a perfectly executed kick or a successful read of an opponent's play, he found a thread of comfort weaving through his nerves.

As Andy dedicated himself to these micro-goals, the crushing anxiety that once stalked him began to fade, replaced by an invigorating excitement for the game. Each moment spent honing his skills shifted his mindset; he was no longer just a competitor weighed down by expectations, but a passionate athlete reveling in the joy of improvement. He began to cherish the process of learning, sharing the court with teammates, and celebrating incremental victories together.

Suddenly, the practice became a sanctuary, a safe haven where he felt less like a performer under scrutiny and more like a growing athlete surrounded by peers who understood the struggles and triumphs of their journey. This environment fostered camaraderie and mutual support, allowing him to remind himself why he fell in love with the game in the first place.

As that change within him ignited a new passion, Andy approached his next match with rejuvenated energy. He was eager to apply the skills he had crafted in practice, ready to embrace the challenge with open arms. Rather than being consumed by fear of failure, he found himself brimming with anticipation for the lessons he would learn, no matter the outcome. The thrill of competition transformed from a daunting specter into a thrilling adventure, and in that moment, he realized that the true essence of sport resided not in the scoreboard, but in the relentless pursuit of personal excellence and the joy of the journey itself.

DEVELOPING A PRE-PERFORMANCE ROUTINE

Crafting a tailored pre-performance routine can provide a comforting sense of control, easing the usual tension that bubbles up before competitions. By establishing familiar rituals, athletes can channel their nerves into focus, transforming anxiety into a grounded readiness that allows them to shine in the moment.

In the world of competitive gymnastics, where bright lights and roaring crowds could drown out even the most determined spirit, Ellen discovered something magical: the power of a personalized pre-performance routine. It was her anchor in the storm of anxiety.

Each time she stepped into the gym, she followed the familiar sequence she had crafted just for herself. First, she'd lace up her shoes, the tightness around her ankles a comforting reminder of the strength she carried within. She'd begin with gentle warm-up exercises, moving her body through stretches and rhythmic motions, shaking out the tension from her limbs and breathing deeply, inhaling confidence.

As beads of sweat formed on her brow, Ellen whispered her positive affirmations: "I am prepared. I am focused." The words rolled off her tongue like a well-worn mantra, each syllable fortifying her resolve and grounding her in the present moment. She could feel the heaviness of doubt beginning to lift, replaced by a warmth that swirled inside her like a newly ignited flame.

Then, in the sanctuary of her mind, she delved into a world of visualization. Closing her eyes, she conjured up images of her routines — the graceful leaps, the flawless flips, the nameless exhilaration of conquering her fears. Her favorite songs played softly in the background, their melodies wrapping around her like a comforting embrace, the rhythm syncing with her heartbeat as she imagined each move flowing effortlessly.

In those precious moments, Ellen transformed her pre-competition jitters into a wellspring of focus. With every note and every visual, she locked in on the task at hand, solidifying her resolve to take the stage and shine. The noise of the outside world faded away, leaving only the sweet sound of her own heartbeat and the unwavering belief that she was ready for whatever came next.

Incorporating stress management techniques into the training routines of young athletes is a game changer, not just for their performance, but for their emotional well-being. Imagine a soccer player, barely twelve, overwhelmed by the pressure to win as the crowd's roar fills the air. By teaching these young athletes to recognize their stressors and symptoms—like tight shoulders or racing hearts—they can learn to navigate these feelings rather than be controlled by them.

In the quiet moments before practice, coaches can introduce simple relaxation techniques—deep breathing, visualization, or even a few minutes of mindfulness—to help them find their center again. And just as importantly, creating an environment that encourages open communication allows athletes to express their fears and anxieties freely.

As these strategies become part of their routine, young athletes transform, building resilience that doesn't just help them on the field, but in life. They learn to enjoy the sport, not just chase the win, discovering their true potential along the way. Through this journey, they realize that managing stress is just as vital as mastering their skills; it's about thriving, not just surviving, and finding joy in the game they love.

THE IMPACT OF TEAM DYNAMICS ON YOUNG ATHLETES

In the realm of youth sports, the scoreboard tells only part of the story. Beyond the high-fives and the cheering crowds lies a rich tapestry where competition intertwines with the nuances of human connection. Here, young athletes are not merely refining their skills; they are embarking on a journey through a landscape of friendships, rivalries, and self-discovery.

This chapter dives into the intricate dance of team dynamics—how friendships blossom and fray under the pressure of practices and games, how coaches become mentors or hurdles depending on their approach, and how conflicts can spark growth or division. We'll explore the challenges these young players face as they build their identities on and off the field, learning to communicate, make decisions, and resolve conflicts in ways that will echo through their lives long after the final whistle blows. It's a world where every pass, every cheer, and every heartache contributes to a larger narrative of resilience and growth.

PEER RELATIONSHIPS AND PERFORMANCE

In the world of youth sports, the bonds formed—or broken—on the field can shape an athlete's experience in profound ways. Picture a soccer team buzzing with energy, where laughter and banter mix with the adrenaline of competition. These moments are more than just casual interactions; they are the threads that weave young players' identities. When teammates uplift one another, offering encouragement and camaraderie, it fuels a sense of belonging. This buoyant atmosphere, as revealed in a study by Smith et al. (2019), can spark a fire of motivation inside young athletes, boosting their self-esteem and pushing them to strive for greatness.

Yet, the landscape isn't always friendly. Rivalries can creep in like a shadow, turning practice into a battleground instead of a play-ground. When competition turns sour, it can breed anxiety and self-doubt, chipping away at a player's confidence. The pressure to outperform others takes root, often stunting their growth both on and off the field. This delicate balance of friendships and rival-ries shapes the course of their athletic journey—one moment filled with laughter, the next with tension, and ultimately crafting the narrative of who they are as athletes and as individuals.

THE RIVALRY OF DANIEL AND JERRY

On a youth soccer team where talent reigned, Daniel and Jerry stood out as the shining stars. Both their skills were undeniable, yet the tension between them crackled like static—two forces constantly vying for supremacy. Daniel was the kind of player who thrived in a chorus, his bright energy lifting others; he was quick to cheer on a teammate or lend a hand after a tough tackle. In contrast, Jerry was laser-focused on outperforming Daniel, his keen eyes trained on the scoreboard rather than the faces of his fellow players.

But everything changed during the regionals when fate's cruel hand struck. A sudden injury sidelined Daniel, leaving him to watch from the sidelines as his team prepared to face their biggest rivals. Jerry now found himself in a position he hadn't anticipated—he wasn't just playing for himself anymore; he had to rally the team without their ever-encouraging cornerstone.

With Daniel's absence echoing in the air, Jerry stumbled through moments of uncertainty, casting glances toward the empty spot where his rival usually stood. However, as the game unfolded, he realized he had the chance to shift gears. He let go of the relentless pursuit to outshine Daniel and began to weave himself into the fabric of the team. Encouraging passes, celebrating defensive plays, and even offering a hand to a struggling teammate became his new normal.

The first whistle blew as if announcing a transformation, and with Jerry's newfound approach, the team began to flourish. What had once felt fragmented evolved into a symphony of movement, each player stepping in rhythm, building one another up. That day, they didn't just play soccer; they wove a bond strong enough to withstand their fiercest opponents.

As the clock ticked down, the game culminated in an adrenaline-filled finale, the scoreboard lighting up with their victory. In the ecstatic aftermath, Jerry turned to see Daniel on the sidelines, a proud smile stretched across his face. It didn't take long for Jerry to realize that their rivalry had turned into something far richer— a camaraderie that uplifted every single player on their team.

Through the journey from competition to cooperation, Jerry had not only transformed his approach to the game but also the dynamics of the team. In the end, they didn't just triumph over their rivals; they learned the true power of unity and friendship, the kind that could ignite any field they stood upon.

COACHING STYLES AND PSYCHOLOGICAL DEVELOPMENT

The essence of coaching goes beyond teaching skills; it's about nurturing the minds and spirits of young athletes. In the world of competition, a coach's style can profoundly influence not just how a team performs, but how its members see themselves.

Some coaches lead with an iron fist, their voices echoing like thunder on the field, barking commands and pushing for immediate results. Sure, their players might dash down the pitch with adrenaline coursing through their veins, but what lies beneath that surface? Each command, each scowl, chips away at the joy of the game, replacing it with a tense urgency. The resilience they build feels more like a fragile shield, tucked away in the shadows, hidden behind the pressure to perform. In the end, the love for the sport often dims, leaving players running not for the thrill of the game, but out of fear of disappointment.

Then there's the democratic style, where encouragement rather than commands takes center stage. Coaches who engage their athletes in conversation, and who listen as much as they lead, create an environment where young players feel seen and heard. Research by Côté & Fraser-Thomas (2007) highlights that this supportive atmosphere not only bolsters emotional engagement but also acts as a balm for anxiety, allowing athletes to thrive.

And let's not forget the permissive approach, which can sometimes resemble a free-for-all. While it grants freedom, without guidance, young athletes may flounder, lost in a sea of choices without a compass. The result can be confusion, and although the intention is to promote autonomy, a lack of structure can leave them vulnerable.

COACH MIKE'S APPROACH

Coach Mike had a knack for bringing out the best in his players, and it all started with his unique approach to leadership. He believed in the power of democracy on the field, inviting each of his athletes to share their voices and insights. This wasn't just a game to him; it was a team, a family—one where everyone's opinion mattered.

When the team suffered a crushing defeat, rather than pointing fingers or laying blame, Coach Mike gathered everyone for an open discussion. The locker room, usually filled with the echoes of laughter and banter, grew quiet as players started to voice their thoughts. He listened intently, creating a safe harbor where they could express their frustrations and fears, the pain of the loss hanging in the air like a thick fog.

Together, they dissected the game, exploring what went wrong and brainstorming new strategies. The atmosphere transformed from one of despair to a renewed sense of purpose. It wasn't just about tactics; it was about building resilience. Coach Mike's guidance didn't just turn their game around; it instilled in them a belief in their own strength to face any challenge. The lessons they learned went far beyond the court, shaping not only skilled athletes but also unwavering individuals ready to tackle whatever life threw their way.

SOCIAL IDENTITY AND TEAM BELONGINGNESS

The feeling of being part of a team can shape not just an athlete's skills, but their very sense of self. Picture a young soccer player, standing on the field painted with the vibrant colors of their team: the thrill of wearing their jersey, the camaraderie shared with teammates, and the communal hopes pinned on each game.

This connection isn't just about strategy or training; it's about identity.

Social identity theory, developed by Tajfel and Turner, sheds light on this phenomenon. It suggests that we draw a portion of who we are from the groups we belong to. For these young athletes, being part of a team can ignite a fire within—fueling their motivation, building their confidence, and deepening their commitment to the sport. When they see themselves as more than just individuals, but as key pieces of a larger puzzle, their passion for the game swells. They play not just for personal glory, but for the pride of their team, creating bonds and dreams that often last far beyond the final whistle.

Feeling connected to a team fosters resilience during challenging times. It's like being stitched together with unseen threads—a shared purpose that pulls everyone a little closer. For instance, research by Steffens and colleagues in 2017 uncovered something remarkable: when a team embraces a strong sense of identity, its members are more likely to dig deeper and push through adversity. It's not just about individual grit; it's about how, together, they find strength in unity when the going gets tough.

THE POWER OF BELONGING

When Olivia first stepped onto the pool deck, the echoes of laughter and splashes felt like a distant melody, one she hadn't quite learned to dance to. She watched from the sidelines, her heart racing as her introverted nature held her back. Each practice felt like a test—one where the confidence of her teammates shone brightly, while she struggled to find her place.

But as the weeks slipped by, something shifted. The relays began to weave a thread of connection among them, each swimmer pulling together in that thrilling race against time. In those moments, Olivia found warmth in the camaraderie, her team-mates leaning in to cheer her on, their voices ringing with encouragement. She started to open up, sharing tentative jokes and moments of vulnerability, and in return, she received smiles that anchored her, making the chaos of competition feel a little less daunting.

As her friendships blossomed, so did her confidence. With each stroke in the water, she felt lighter, faster—her times began to reflect the hard work and passion she tucked away beneath her quiet exterior. No longer just a solitary swimmer, Olivia transformed into a vital part of the team, her laughter mingling with theirs, a vibrant note in their shared story.

Through this journey, the water wasn't just a place for practice; it became her haven, a space where she felt truly seen and accepted. With renewed strength and unwavering support, Olivia stepped off the blocks not only as a swimmer who had improved her strokes but as a teammate who had found her voice, embodying what it truly meant to belong.

ROLE OF COMMUNICATION

In the world of sports, where every play counts and every moment is layered with tension, it's the conversations off the field that often set the stage for success. Coaches and athletes learn quickly that effective communication isn't just a nice-to-have; it's the backbone of a team that feels secure and valued. It's in those candid discussions, where thoughts are shared and opinions welcomed, that psychological safety flourishes. When every voice is heard, teams don't just perform better; they grow stronger together. Research backs this up, revealing that the way team members communicate can shape their unity and, ultimately, their performance outcomes (Distefano et al., 2018). In this tight-knit environment, every exchange—whether it's a pep talk before a game or a debriefing afterward—plays a crucial role in weaving a culture of trust and support.

THE VOICE OF THE TEAM

In the heat of the championship game, the tension buzzed like static in the air, but something felt off. As the ball zipped from player to player, it was clear: they weren't on the same wavelength. Frustration flickered in their eyes as chances slipped through their fingers—passes that went unanswered and plays that fell flat.

Coach Kevan, ever the observer, called for a timeout. He paced the sideline, fingers entwined, and looked each player square in the eye. "You need to talk to one another. Without communication, this team is just a collection of individuals. We need signals, explicit calls, something we can all rely on."

It didn't take long for the words to sink in. At practice, they began to experiment with hand signals and loud calls, each player growing more confident as they practiced aloud. The first time Alex called out the play with enthusiasm, the rest of the team responded instinctively, an unspoken understanding forming, threading them tighter together.

As the days turned into weeks, those practice sessions bore fruit. The players carried that newfound synergy into games, each play unfolding with a clarity they hadn't had before. They cheered one another on, their voices rising in a chorus that echoed off the walls. The missed chances slowly transformed into triumphant scores, frustration blossoming into trust, and what had once been five strangers on the court morphed into a family, rooted in the language they crafted together.

IMPACT OF GROUP DYNAMICS ON DECISION-MAKING

In the world of youth sports, the interplay of group dynamics can profoundly influence how young athletes make decisions, especially when the heat of competition bears down on them. Research by Vallerand and colleagues in 2006 reveals that when a team operates in a positive environment, where support and camaraderie flourish, athletes are better equipped to tackle challenges together. Conversely, when toxic dynamics seep into the team atmosphere, they can stifle performance, leaving athletes struggling to rise above the pressure. In these moments, it becomes clear: the strength of the team can make or break a young athlete's spirit and success.

THE PRESSURE OF THE PLAYOFFS

The championship game loomed like a storm on the horizon, and the air buzzed with anticipation. As the clock ticked closer to the final minutes, the team found themselves at a crossroads, caught in a tense discussion about their offensive strategy.

It was a moment steeped in uncertainty, but their bond—formed through countless hours of practice and shared victories—was palpable. Each player's voice echoed in that huddle, grounded in respect and trust. They gathered together, the echoes of their laughter and camaraderie from the season infusing the atmosphere with a rare clarity.

"Should we stick to what we know?" one player asked, glancing around at his teammates. The question resonated: they had poured their hearts into this game throughout the season.

Another chimed in, emboldened by their collective energy. "But what if we surprise them? We can adapt, play off each other's strengths."

They listened, weighing the pros and cons, knowing that every word mattered in that crucial decision. With no one overshadowing the group, they navigated that moment like a well-rehearsed play, absorbing each perspective until a consensus emerged—a bold new approach, one that could set them apart from the opposition.

As they re-entered the game, there was a spark in their eyes, a mix of anxiety and excitement. The shift had solidified their unity, and it quickly paid off, their new strategy weaving through the defense like a shot of adrenaline. The crowd held its breath, and when that final whistle blew, it marked not just a victory on the scoreboard, but a testament to the power of their collaboration—a reminder that when a team thrives on trust and shared intention, anything is possible.

LONG-TERM OUTCOMES OF TEAM EXPERIENCES

The dynamics experienced in youth sports is a vibrant tapestry woven with lessons that extend far beyond the playing field. The bonds formed during those formative years often leave indelible marks on relationships and career choices later in life. A team that celebrates victories and navigates losses together teaches invaluable lessons in teamwork, leadership, and conflict resolution—skills that are as crucial in the boardroom as they are on the field.

Research by Gould et al. (2008) echoes this sentiment, revealing that young athletes who experience joy and camaraderie in their sports endeavors tend to carry that positivity into adulthood. These individuals develop remarkable resilience and adaptability, traits that empower them to confront life's challenges with confidence and grace. The echoes of those youthful games linger on, shaping not just the athletes they become, but the lives they touch.

BRIDGING INTO ADULTHOOD

Years later, at a charity event bathed in soft, golden light, Valentina found herself in the company of her old swimming teammates. Each of them had carved their own unique paths through the currents of life, but here, in this moment, they were united by shared memories and an enduring bond. As Valentina surveyed the room, she couldn't help but feel a swell of nostalgia.

Now a thriving psychotherapist, she recalled the lessons learned in the water—the rhythm of teamwork and the strength in vulnerability. These principles had woven themselves into her practice, guiding her through the delicate dance of therapy. With every client, she emphasized the necessity of collaboration and open dialogue, the very same dynamics that had propelled her and her teammates forward in the pool.

Laughter bubbled up like water splashing at the pool's edge, filling the air with warmth and familiarity. Valentina's heart swelled as she witnessed the ease with which they fell back into conversation, reminiscing about early morning practices and shared triumphs. In that moment, her newfound purpose shone brightly, a luminous thread connecting their childhood camaraderie with the complexities of their adult lives. The echoes of their past blended with the present, reminding them all that even as they floated along different paths, they remained forever tethered by the currents of friendship.

The world of young athletes is not just about the game; it's a complex tapestry woven with threads of camaraderie, resilience, and growth. Each practice session becomes a shared adventure where friendships are forged and life lessons are learned amid the drills and scrimmages. The bond that forms among teammates transcends mere skills; it's about trust, support, and the collective joy of striving toward a common goal.

Coaches and parents often fixate on the scoreboard, but the true magic happens in the warmth of teamwork. Encouraging a culture of inclusion and open communication helps shape not only skilled athletes but also well-rounded individuals. A nurturing environment allows young athletes to find their voices, learn the value of collaboration, and handle both triumphs and setbacks with grace.

When we recognize how vital these interpersonal dynamics are, we pave the way for our young athletes to thrive—not just on the field, but in every aspect of their lives. By fostering a sense of belonging and understanding, we prepare them for success that reverberates far beyond the final whistle. This is where the real game begins.

THE INTERSECTION OF IDENTITY AND ATHLETICS

DEFINING IDENTITY IN SPORTS

Identity is a complex tapestry, woven from the threads of our experiences, beliefs, and the roles we play in the lives of others. For young athletes, the field or court becomes more than just a place to compete; it transforms into a vital space where their sense of self begins to take shape. Through the lens of social identity theory, we see that much of who we are is linked to the groups we belong to, a concept highlighted by scholars like Tajfel and Turner back in '86. In the world of sports, being an athlete isn't just a title; it's a badge of honor that boosts self-esteem and colors the way athletes engage with their peers and the world around them. Each game played, each practice endured, reinforces that identity, turning a simple sport into a powerful tool for self-definition and connection.

MACKENZIE

Mackenzie had always been the kind of girl who thrived in circles of camaraderie. In high school, her laughter blended seamlessly with her friends' as they swapped secrets and shared dreams. When they coaxed her into joining the cross-country team, it felt natural—just another way to cement those bonds. But what began as a casual way to hang out soon evolved into something altogether different.

As the days turned into weeks, and weeks turned into months, Mackenzie found herself drawn deeper into the rhythm of running. The pounding of her feet against the earth became a heartbeat of its own, resonating with an energy she never knew she craved. Each morning, as dawn spilled gold across the sky, she laced up her worn sneakers, and the world faded away. It was just her, the track, and the pulse of her body—powerful and alive.

"I'm a runner," she would tell anyone who asked, her voice tinged with the pride that had blossomed within her. It wasn't just a label; it was an anthem of her identity. Each race, each challenge, carved out a space for her that was separate from grades and GPA. She reveled in the exhilarating sense of buoyancy that running offered, feeling strong and capable in a way that was distinct from her successes in the classroom.

Research suggests that young athletes like Mackenzie undergo a transformative process, where the lessons learned on the field shape their self-image and values. With every step on the trail, she was reaffirming her worth, building an identity grounded in sweat and grit. Her aspirations began to shift, fueled by the drive to be more than just a student. She wasn't merely running; she was discovering who she was on a profound level, one mile at a time.

CULTURAL INFLUENCES ON SPORT PARTICIPATION

Cultural backgrounds shape the choices, motivations, and identities of young athletes in profound ways. For many, sports become more than just a pastime; they transform into a canvas for cultural expression. Through the lens of competition and teamwork, these young athletes explore who they are, blending their dreams of athletic success with the rich narratives of their heritage. As they sprint across fields and court the thrill of victory, they also navigate the complexities of their identities, weaving their passions into the fabric of their cultural stories. In this intricate dance of sport and self, they uncover not just their potential as athletes, but also the depth of their unique backgrounds, ultimately forging a path that honors both their heritage and their aspirations.

Leonardo stood at the edge of the field, the vibrant green grass stretching before him like an invitation. He could hear the laughter of his friends as they kicked the ball to one another, the thrill of the game calling out to him like a siren's song. Yet, in the back of his mind, his parents' voices echoed, heavy with the weight of their cultural expectations.

"Focus on your studies, Leonardo. Sports won't get you anywhere," they would remind him, their accents thick with the sound of home. It had become a mantra, one that created a rift within him—a battleground between his passion for soccer and the desire to honor his family's sacrifices.

Each day after school, he found himself at that field, heart racing with the joy of the game, all the while feeling the pull of his responsibilities. His friends would often tease him, "Come on, Leo, just play! You're too good to sit on the sidelines!" Yet, guilt would wash over him, reminding him of the countless hours his parents dedicated to giving him opportunities they never had.

One afternoon, as the sun hung low and painted the sky in hues of orange and pink, he decided to sit his parents down. He took a deep breath, his palms sweaty as he conveyed his feelings—how soccer wasn't just a game for him; it was a piece of his identity, a way to connect with the community around him, and a bridge to his heritage. The joy he felt when he scored a goal or assisted a teammate was unmatched, and it motivated him in his academic pursuits.

His father listened, nodding slowly, while his mother, initially reluctant, began to soften as she recognized the importance of balance in his life. With each word, Leonardo could see the walls shifting; the conversation became a dance of understanding and compromise.

Days turned into weeks, and slowly, his parents began to see soccer through his eyes. They attended his games, standing on the sidelines, clapping, cheering, and even learning some of the chants that echoed from the crowd.

In those moments, Leonardo discovered an unexpected joy—the amalgamation of his two worlds. Soccer became a way to honor his roots, where the rhythm of the game blended seamlessly with the pulse of his heritage. He learned that cultural identity wasn't a barrier but a source of strength, inspiring him on the field and in the classroom.

As he raced down the field, feeling the wind whip through his hair, Leonardo understood that he no longer had to choose between the two. He could be a student, a son, and a soccer player all at once, thriving in a vibrant space where dreams and responsibilities met. In embracing both sides of his life, he found a harmony that propelled him forward—a celebration of who he was, rooted in culture and driven by passion.

Studies show that cultural identity can be a powerful motivator for young athletes, providing them with a sense of strength and purpose rooted in their heritage (Baker & Côté, 2003). When these young competitors step onto the field or court, they carry not just their own dreams, but the hopes and stories of their ancestors, infusing their efforts with a deeper significance that drives them to excel.

THE PSYCHOLOGICAL TOLL OF COMPETITION

While sports offer profound benefits, the bright lights of competition often mask the shadows lurking just beneath the surface. For young athletes, the thrill of the game can quickly turn into a battleground of pressure and expectations. Each practice, each game, becomes not just a test of skill but a crucible for their self-worth.

In the locker room, laughter melds with the tension, as players put on brave faces while grappling with a gnawing anxiety. The fear of letting down their coaches, their teammates, and themselves can feel like an anvil resting on their chests. It's a silent struggle, where the thrill of victory is coveted, yet the stakes can feel unbearably high. For many, the lines between who they are and how they perform on the field blur until they're indistinguishable, leaving them caught in a paradox—where success can sometimes sour into a sense of failure, and validation from peers becomes the yardstick for their identity.

In the end, what should be a celebration of talent and teamwork can morph into a complex web of expectations, revealing the quiet, often unseen psychological challenges faced by those just trying to play the game they love.

Vakare had always been a standout on the track, each race seemingly effortless as she breezed past her competitors. High school had become a whirlwind of victories and accolades, a golden era where her dreams of becoming a top-tier athlete felt within reach. But as the stakes rose, so did the weight on her shoulders.

In the quiet moments before a race, she felt the thrum of anxiety take hold, knotting her stomach in a way that left her breathless.

Every stride she took was now punctuated by the fear of letting someone down—her coaches, her teammates, and most hauntingly, herself. It was a reality she had never prepared for, a shadow lurking behind the glory.

One afternoon, she found herself sitting across from her coach in the small, sun-drenched office that had seen countless athletes before her. The words tumbled out, unrestrained, as she opened up about her fears—how she felt like a tightly wound spring ready to snap, how each race felt like a judgment of her worth. "What if I can't keep this up?" she confessed, vulnerability lacing her voice. "What if I fail?"

Her coach listened intently, the weight of her words resonating. It was a familiar struggle, one echoed in the research that studied the complex relationship between self-esteem and performance in young athletes, illuminating how easily passion could tilt into distress (Gould et al., 2006). As Vakare spoke, it dawned on her that her identity had become entwined with her athletic prowess, and that realization felt both liberating and terrifying.

The conversation shifted, her coach reminding her that while winning mattered, it didn't define her. It was in that exchange that Vakare glimpsed a new perspective, understanding that her worth was rooted in more than just her speed—it was embedded in her courage to face her fears. As she left the office, a flicker of hope ignited within her, a reminder that the race wasn't just about the finish line but the journey of discovering who she was beneath all the pressure.

ROLE OF COACHES AND MENTORSHIP

Coaches and mentors are vital in helping young athletes confront the complexities of their identities. With thoughtful guidance, effective coaching not only enhances athletic skills but also nurtures emotional well-being, fostering a balanced growth that acknowledges the multifaceted nature of their lives. By prioritizing a holistic approach, these mentors create an environment where young competitors can thrive both on and off the field, learning to embrace who they are in every aspect of their journey.

Aiden had always put everything he had into basketball. It was more than a game; it was his passion, his escape. When they lost a critical match that could have catapulted them into the playoffs, it felt like the world had collapsed around him. As he sat in the dimly lit locker room, head hung low, his coach, a seasoned mentor with years of wisdom etched into his face, pulled up a chair beside him.

"Aiden," he started, his voice calm amidst the chaos of emotions swirling in the room. "I know this stings, but listen closely. You are not just a player, and this loss doesn't define you. Every moment on that court is an opportunity. Use it to learn, and everything else will fall into place."

Aiden felt a flicker of hope ignite within him as the coach's words settled in. For so long, he had seen himself as just an athlete—a label that felt both empowering and suffocating. But now, he began to understand that there was more to him than how well he dribbled or shot.

As days turned into weeks, Aiden took those lessons to heart. He embraced his failures, turning each setback into a new chance to grow, both as a player and as a person. With renewed determination, he approached each practice—not just to improve his game, but to unravel the layers of who he truly was. That one game was just a moment in time, a piece of a much larger puzzle he was still learning to complete.

LONG-TERM IMPLICATIONS OF ATHLETIC IDENTITY

Athletic involvement weaves itself into the fabric of our lives in ways we often don't fully grasp until years later. For many, the lessons learned on the field or in the gym trickle into adulthood, quietly crafting our identities. The grit we cultivate, the teamwork we embrace, and the resilience we forge become the guiding principles of our future choices. Whether it's navigating the complexities of a career or building lasting friendships, those early experiences in youth sports lay a foundation that continues to influence who we become. Every sprint, every practice, every moment of triumph or defeat contributes to the narrative of our personal and professional journeys.

Rachel stood at the edge of the pool, the cool blue water shimmering beneath the harsh fluorescent lights. It was in this world of chlorinated lanes and early morning practices that she first learned the importance of discipline and teamwork. Those days of pushing her body to the limit, counting laps, and listening to the rhythmic sound of her breath, shaped her into the resilient woman she would become.

Fast forward several years, and Rachel found herself in a high-stakes boardroom, the weight of the world resting on her shoulders. As a business leader at a global company, she often reflected on her days as a collegiate swimmer. The same principles that guided her in the water now anchored her in the corporate world: meticulous planning, the relentless pursuit of goals, and the invaluable support of her team.

Research suggests that engaging in competitive sports during formative years can instill lifelong skills, nurturing an athletic identity that paves the way for future successes (Weiss & Chaumeton, 1992). For Rachel, those years spent gliding through water were more than just a phase; they were a foundation. Each sprint in the pool had taught her how to strategize, adapt, and thrive under pressure—lessons she now applied to navigating complex business challenges.

As she crafted strategies and rallied her team, Rachel couldn't help but draw parallels. The thrill of competing and the bond she formed with fellow swimmers, all echoed in her current journey, reminding her that whether in a sport or a boardroom, success is seldom a solitary endeavor.

In the world where identity meets athletics isn't just a space filled with wins and losses; it's a nuanced tapestry woven from individual experiences, social influences, gender nuances, cultural backgrounds, and the invaluable support of mentors. By recognizing these intricate layers, we equip coaches, parents, and young athletes with the tools they need to cultivate a nurturing atmosphere—one where identities can thrive. As these young athletes carve out their journeys, they should be inspired to see their involvement in sports not merely as a competition, but as a pathway to personal growth. This journey builds resilience and fosters a multi-dimensional sense of self that extends far beyond the game, shaping the person they are meant to become.

GENDER DIFFERENCES IN ATHLETIC EXPERIENCES

The realm of competitive sports encompasses a diverse array of psychological experiences, shaped profoundly by the norms and expectations of gender. As we delve into this realm, we begin to see how young athletes—boys and girls alike—forge their paths through the unique challenges and pressures they face. This chapter explores the rich tapestry of their experiences, revealing how societal expectations and stereotypes impact their mental resilience. We'll look at the role of coaching styles, the importance of support systems, and the growing awareness around mental health, all framed within the intensity of competition. By examining these factors, we gain deeper insight into the ways young athletes confront their struggles and triumphs in the arena of sports, offering a nuanced understanding of their journeys.

PSYCHOLOGICAL RESILIENCE AND GENDER

In the world of young athletes, societal expectations and gender norms weave an intricate tapestry that can shape their resilience and mental toughness. Boys are often lauded for their grit, while girls are pushed to maintain a delicate balance between strength and grace. This balancing act creates a pressure cooker environment, where the expectations of coaches, peers, and families mingle with the athletes' own aspirations.

As they train, they encounter not just physical challenges, but the weight of stereotypes that dictate how they should behave, compete, and even celebrate their victories. For the boys, it means toughing it out and showing little emotion, while the girls are often expected to smile and be gracious, even in defeat. These societal scripts can either forge unbreakable spirits or leave them feeling like they're always one step behind.

In the heat of competition, each athlete must navigate these precarious waters, where their sense of self-worth often hinges on meeting these external demands. With every hurdle cleared, or every goal scored, they learn to adapt, to push past the limitations set by others, and to redefine what it means to be strong on their own terms. It's in these moments of struggle and triumph that they cultivate a resilience that goes far beyond the playing field— one that prepares them for life's broader challenges, teaching them that true toughness isn't just about winning, but about staying true to themselves amidst the turmoil of expectation.

In a world where the roar of the crowd is typically reserved for boys, Veronica, a 15-year-old soccer player, finds herself navigating an arena filled with skepticism and doubt. Clad in her worn cleats, she hits the pitch in a league dominated by boys, fueled by an unyielding passion for the game — a passion deemed unconventional by everyone around her. Raised in a culture that whispers, "Soccer is for boys," Veronica faces not just her opponents but the weight of societal expectations, pushing back against the tide of disbelief that threatens to swallow her determination.

Each practice is a battle, yet it forges a resilience within her that goes far beyond athletic prowess. The bruises on her legs and the sweat dripping from her brow are mere markers of her physical struggles; the true challenge lies in dismantling the narrow beliefs of what girls can achieve. As she fiercely dribbles past defenders, Veronica isn't just proving her worth on the field; she's rewriting the narrative for herself and for others who dare to challenge the status quo.

Research by McCarthy et al. (2019) indicates that young female athletes like Veronica, facing gender-based skepticism, often emerge stronger and more resilient as they confront the barriers in their paths. With every goal scored, with every naysayer silenced, her journey becomes one of defiance, turning those societal whispers into a symphony of empowerment, proving that passion knows no gender. In her eyes, the beautiful game is not just a sport; it's a stage for rebellion, resilience, and the relentless pursuit of her dreams.

In contrast, Richard, a gifted basketball player with a towering presence on the court, feels the weight of expectation pressing down on him like a heavy jersey. Every dribble echoes a demand to outshine his teammates, to embody the tough-guy persona that seems to define male sports culture. It's a role he struggles to fit into, the notion that real men shouldn't show weakness gnawing at him inside.

As he trains, the thrill of the game is often overshadowed by creeping anxiety, the burden of needing to be invincible, to always push through the pain without a hint of doubt. He remembers a time when expressing how he felt didn't feel like such a burden – those moments seem so distant now.

Studies have shown that many male athletes internalize this relentless drive for toughness, an expectation that only fuels their anxiety rather than alleviating it (O'Donnell et al., 2020).

In this world, resilience manifests differently for Richard and his female counterparts. For him, it's about concealing the storm within, while for them, it often centers on breaking through the barriers that hold them back. Both are heroes in their own right, yet the pressures that shape their journeys rarely mirror each other, highlighting the complicated landscape of modern athletics.

COACHING STYLES AND GENDER IMPACT

Coaching plays a pivotal role in shaping the growth of athletes, yet the influence of gender perceptions can quietly reshape this dynamic. Studies reveal that coaches frequently adjust their approach depending on whether an athlete is male or female, subtly affecting motivation, self-esteem, and the likelihood of sticking with the sport. In the world of competition, these seemingly small shifts can have lasting repercussions on the journeys of young athletes as they navigate their passion for the game.

In the dimly lit wrestling gym, the air thick with the scent of sweat and determination, Tyler, a sixteen-year-old with a fierce competitive spirit, grappled not just with his opponents but with the demanding weight of his coach's expectations. Coach Ramirez was a force of nature — a relentless taskmaster whose approach was steeped in traditional, authoritarian methods. He believed in pushing his athletes to their limits, in cultivating aggression as a means to forge champions.

Under Coach Ramirez's watchful eye, Tyler felt an adrenaline-fueled surge of confidence each time he stepped onto the mat, the thrill of competition coursing through him. But as the season progressed, the pressure mounted like the layers of his heavy singlet, each match turning into a test of will and strength, and with every expected victory, a whisper of self-doubt crept in when he stumbled.

Expectations hung over him like a storm cloud, heavy and oppressive, and he wrestled with the unsettling fear of failure that lingered just at the edges of his mind. Every practice pushed him harder, but with it came the nagging question: What if he didn't measure up? Each victory felt like a fragile triumph, ready to shatter under the weight of tomorrow's demands.

This method can build a solid sense of confidence, yet it often comes with a weighty side effect: the burden of unrealistically high expectations. When those expectations aren't met, self-doubt can creep in, leaving individuals questioning their abilities and choices (Gilbert & Trudel, 2004).

Conversely, female athletes like Vivian, a spirited 14-year-old gymnast, had always thrived in environments where support and teamwork reigned. Her old coach, with a warm smile and an understanding ear, fostered a sense of belonging among the girls, encouraging them to voice their fears and dreams alike. Practices were filled with laughter as much as drills, and it felt less like pressure and more like a community dedicated to growth.

But everything shifted when Vivian joined a new gymnastics team, one that bore the fierce intensity of competition at its core. The coach, known for his strict methods and no-nonsense attitude, ruled the gym with an iron fist. The once-welcoming space suddenly felt suffocating, with sharp words echoing off the walls and the pressure to perform crushing her spirit. As Vivian stood on the edge of the mat, heart racing and palms sweating, the camaraderie she cherished slipped away, leaving behind a raw sense of isolation.

In this unforgiving atmosphere, the struggles began to mount. Where once there was confidence buoyed by encouragement, now nagging doubts wormed their way into her thoughts. Adjusting to this new reality proved to be a monumental challenge, and with each passing day, Vivian found herself battling not

just the routines, but also the creeping tide of diminished motivation and a slowly unraveling sense of self-worth. The joy of
gymnastics, once a beacon of light, was now overshadowed by the
weight of expectation.

GENDER STEREOTYPES IN SPORTS

Gender stereotypes continue to shape participation and self-
concept among young athletes. These stereotypes often dictate
the type of sports deemed "appropriate" for each gender, leading
to young athletes like Sophie, a twelve-year-old with a fierce love
for football, every tick of the clock felt amplified.

Sophie stood by the goalpost, shivering slightly despite the
summer heat, her signature ponytail swinging as she practiced her
kicks. The boys on her team called her "Soph," their tone a mix of
camaraderie and disbelief. But at school, when the cafeteria
buzzed with laughter, the whispers wrapped around her like a
suffocating blanket. "What are you doing, playing a boys' sport?"
floated from the corner table where the popular girls conjoined,
their judgment thinly veiled by giggles.

While some girls slipped into the roles society had laid out for
them, Sophie wrestled with an invisible weight. Each time she
donned her cleats, she wasn't just stepping onto the field; she was
stepping out of the confines of expectation. Shadows of doubt
crept into her mind, fueling her with both determination and a
nagging uncertainty. Could she claim her place in the sport
without losing herself in the process?

Despite the ridicule, Sophie felt a surge of pride every time she
scored a goal or made a perfect pass. Yet, the triumph was often
marred by her inner battle—should she hide her passion to fit in,
or could she carve her own path without sacrificing the friendships she desperately wanted? The struggle between embracing

her identity and yearning for acceptance danced in her mind like a finely tuned playbook.

As the season progressed, Sophie found herself more resilient, her confidence growing with each practice and game. The whispers faded, replaced by louder cheers from teammates who recognized her talent, her laughter blending with theirs. In those moments, Sophie's blend of joy and conflict painted a portrait of a young athlete not just defying stereotypes, but redefining what it meant to belong.

On the other hand, Johnny, an 11-year-old dancer with a passion for pirouettes and pliés, felt the weight of the world bearing down on him. He loved the way the music wrapped around him like a warm embrace, the thrill of each performance lighting up his soul. But with each turn and leap, he also carried the heavy burden of needing to prove himself. Dance was often seen as a feminine pursuit, and that perception loomed over him like a storm cloud.

As he laced up his ballet shoes, Johnny couldn't shake the feeling that he had to justify his love for the art. Why should he have to? He thought about the boys at school who laughed and whispered behind his back, dismissing his dreams as something frivolous. The pressure to fit into the box of what boys "should" do gnawed at him. He was caught in a tug-of-war between embracing his passion and conforming to the rigid expectations of gender norms that dictated what was acceptable for boys like him.

Research by Eagly & Wood (1999) echoed in his mind, illuminating a harsh reality: the stereotypes surrounding masculinity painted a picture of aggression and competition, which often led boys like Johnny to shy away from pursuits like dance. He recognized that he wasn't alone; many young boys felt the same pull toward activities deemed "feminine," but the fear of being judged kept them at bay. Johnny took a deep breath, reminding himself that his love for dance was just as valid as any sport, no matter what anyone else thought. In that moment, he resolved to embrace his passion fully, no matter the odds stacked against him.

MENTAL HEALTH TRENDS

The mental health landscape among young athletes reveals distinct trends correlated with gender. Anxiety and depression, often exacerbated by performance pressure and body image concerns, affect athletes differently. Female athletes are particularly susceptible to body image issues, driven in part by societal portrayals of femininity tied to appearance (McLean et al., 2015).

Take Amber, for example—a 16-year-old swimmer whose life revolves around the rhythmic splashes of water and the thrill of racing her peers. Amber is driven by her love for the pool, but beneath the surface lies a current of anxiety that threatens to drown her passion. The pressure to excel can feel suffocating, especially as she scrolls through social media, bombarded by images of what society deems the "ideal" athlete.

Amber often finds herself measuring her worth against the sleek, toned bodies of her competitors, each comparison deepening her sense of inadequacy. She knows she should be focused on her strokes, on perfecting her flip turns, but instead, she gets caught in the grip of self-doubt, her body image looming larger than any victory could ever feel.

In her pursuit of excellence, Amber realizes that the joy of swimming is often eclipsed by a relentless quest for an unattainable ideal, transforming her love for the sport into a cycle of anxiety and dissatisfaction. Through her story, it becomes painfully clear that while the lanes of the pool may be clear, the waters of mental well-being are often murky and fraught with challenges, especially for young women like her.

Conversely, male athletes like Ethan, a 14-year-old football player, stood on the sidelines, his heart racing as he watched his teammates train under the glaring afternoon sun. The weight of expectations pressed down on him—his own, as well as those of his coaches and peers. It wasn't just the competition that gnawed at him; it was the relentless demand to embody an ideal of masculinity that felt both suffocating and unattainable. He could feel the anxiety curling around him like smoke, unseen yet all-consuming.

In the locker room, the unspoken rules were clear: vulnerability was a weakness, and mental health was a topic reserved for whispers, if mentioned at all. The stigma loomed like a heavy fog, making it nearly impossible for Ethan to voice the struggles that twisted in his gut. He was too often caught in a battle—facing the pressure to perform while keeping his feelings locked away. The untreated anxiety simmered beneath the surface, influencing his every move on the field, and jeopardizing not just his game but his sense of self. And as he laced up his cleats week after week, the fear of failure loomed larger than the actual threat of the next big play.

Boys often find themselves trapped in silence when it comes to mental health. The unspoken rules, the weight of expectations, and the fear of judgment can make it seem impossible to share what's really going on inside. As a result, many struggle with untreated anxiety and depression, quietly battling their emotions. This internal turmoil doesn't just stay hidden; it spills over into their lives, impacting their performance in school, sports, and friendships, leaving them feeling more isolated than ever (Möller et al., 2017).

COMPETITIVE ENVIRONMENT AND GENDER DIFFERENCES

The competitive landscape between male and female athletes often unfolds in strikingly different ways, each reflecting their unique perspectives on rivalry and camaraderie. Studies indicate that male athletes tend to embrace a more direct form of competition, often thriving on fierce rivalries that push them to their limits (Schember & Boulting, 2011). Take, for example, a boys' soccer team, where the air is thick with the drive to outdo one another; the shouts of players vying for dominance echo across the field, each drill a battleground for individual prowess.

In contrast, female athletes frequently approach competition with a lens of collaboration. Ava's volleyball team is a perfect illustration of this—a collective of friends who bond over shared aspirations. During practice, instead of sharp elbows and harsh words, the atmosphere is filled with encouragement as they set collective goals and support one another's growth. The emphasis isn't just on winning; it's about fostering a sense of unity that extends beyond the court, where the strength of their teamwork becomes their best asset. In this world, competition evolves into a shared journey, reflecting a profound commitment to the success of the group as a whole.

Such contrasting competitive dynamics can shape athletes' experiences. For male athletes, the heat of rivalry ignites a fierce motivation, pushing them to excel, to outperform, and to strive for victory against their peers. It's an adrenaline-fueled race, where the thrill of competition propels them forward.

In stark contrast, female athletes often navigate a different terrain. Here, camaraderie and collaboration are the lifelines. The bonds forged through teamwork enhance their satisfaction, wrapping them in a cocoon of emotional safety that nurtures their spirits. Yet, this divergence in experiences can cast shadows—

moments when comparisons stoke feelings of inadequacy. The subtle undercurrents of competition can stir unease, especially when gender norms amplify perceived gaps in skills or accolades, making the path to achievement feel even more daunting. The weight of these expectations can loom large, affecting how they see themselves and each other in this multifaceted world of sport.

Grasping the nuances of gender differences in athletic experiences is vital for creating a welcoming and nurturing space for young athletes. Each young person brings their own set of emotional struggles, and by recognizing these challenges, we can design interventions that cater to their needs, helping them grow, build resilience, and prioritize their well-being in sports. Coaches, parents, and sports organizations need to actively work towards a culture that honors the distinct journeys of all athletes, moving past outdated gender norms and adopting a more comprehensive understanding of athletic development. As we continue to dismantle barriers and push back against stereotypes, the sports community has the power to uplift every young athlete, enabling them to flourish not just in competition, but in life beyond the field.

PARENTAL INFLUENCE: SUPPORT VS. PRESSURE

In the world of youth sports the scene is alive with energy—children laughing, teammates strategizing, and the thrill of competition hanging in the air. But beneath this vibrant tapestry, there's a complex thread that weaves its way through the fabric of every game and practice: the parents. Their presence can act as a rock-solid foundation, nurturing and cheering from the sidelines, or it can sometimes feel like an anchor, pulling down their young athletes with the weight of unrelenting expectations.

In this charged environment, parents' behaviors echo loudly, shaping the experiences of their children in profound ways. A warm word or a supportive gesture can elevate a young athlete, while a harsh critique can dim their spark, creating a ripple effect on their mental outlook and enjoyment of the game. Navigating the delicate balance of support and pressure is crucial, influencing not just performance but the very essence of what it means to play sports as a young person. Understanding these dynamics is essential for creating a space where kids can thrive and find joy in the journey, regardless of the scoreboard.

DEFINING SUPPORTIVE VS. PRESSURING BEHAVIORS

Supportive parenting creates a nurturing environment where young athletes can blossom, cultivating a deep love for their sport rather than seeking outside approval. Take Sarah, for instance—a spirited ten-year-old soccer player whose enthusiasm for the game thrived under the watchful eyes of her devoted parents. They were a constant presence at her matches, cheering loudly whether she scored a goal or missed a shot, teaching her that every experience on the field was valuable.

After each game, they gathered as a family to chat about what had happened, not in a critical way, but with genuine curiosity about how Sarah felt. Did she enjoy the game? What made her smile? Their conversations were more about her joy than trophy counts, fostering a rich, playful dialogue that made the sport feel like a shared adventure.

In their eyes, success wasn't measured by medals but by the laughter shared during practice or the thrill of a well-played match. Their unwavering support allowed Sarah to flourish—not just as an athlete but as a confident young girl, passionate about the sport she loved. It was this simple yet profound approach that instilled in her an enduring sense of empowerment, reminding her that the game was truly for her, not for anyone else.

On the side of the conflict is John who had always looked up to his father, a once-promising athlete whose dreams of glory had crumbled under the weight of reality. But for John, those dreams felt like a noose tightening around his neck. At twelve, he was already a talented gymnast, and his father's expectations hovered over him like a dark cloud, whispering that he must achieve what his father never could.

Every time John stumbled on a routine—every slight wobble or miscalculated landing—his father's voice pierced through the air, sharp and unyielding. "You've got to do better than that, John. You can't afford to make mistakes." Each critique, though meant to be motivating, felt more like a blade digging deeper into his confidence. The pressure to excel morphed into an invisible weight, heavier with every practice session.

Instead of the thrill of soaring through the air, John found himself gripped by anxiety, his heart racing at the thought of disappointing his father. The glittering gym that had once been a sanctuary began to feel like a cage. Slowly, the love for the sport that had brought him joy began to flicker and fade, replaced by dread. Burnout settled in, and as the smile faded from his face, so too did his desire to compete. The dreams intended to bond father and son now created a chasm between them, leaving John feeling more alone than ever in a sport that had once been his refuge.

The dynamics between athletes and those who support them can make all the difference. According to researchers Smith and Smoll (1996), creating an atmosphere of encouragement significantly boosts athletes' self-esteem and enhances their enjoyment of the game. In contrast, when pressure mounts and expectations weigh heavily, it can lead to feelings of anxiety and an unsettling sense of detachment from the sport. Their work highlights a critical truth: fostering a nurturing environment is essential for healthy participation, while the burden of unrealistic demands can sidetrack an athlete's experience in profoundly negative ways.

IMPACT ON MENTAL ATTITUDES

The impact of parenting styles on an athlete's journey can be both subtle and profound, shaping their mental landscape in unexpected ways. In a world where competition can feel like a high-pressure game, a nurturing environment can be the key to resilience, positivity, and healthy self-esteem.

Take Emma, for instance—a gifted young swimmer with dreams that stretched far beyond the local pool. From a young age, she was enveloped in her mother's unwavering support. Each time Emma dove into the water, she felt her mother's belief in her ability wrapping around her like a comforting warm-up suit. "Swim for joy, not just for medals," her mother would say, and those words echoed in Emma's mind during every race.

When the starting buzzer sounded, Emma no longer saw the competition as a daunting trial. Instead, it was a chance to learn and grow—not just in skill, but in spirit. This perspective, nurtured by her mother's encouragement, didn't just transform the way she swam; it ignited an enduring passion for the sport that would carry her through the ups and downs of her athletic career. Emma learned to embrace each stroke in the water as a step toward something greater than just winning, and that made all the difference.

In the world of competitive sports, pressure can be a double-edged sword, slicing through an athlete's confidence and sense of self. Take Shawn, for instance—a gifted fifteen-year-old tennis player whose dreams of greatness were often overshadowed by the weight of his mother's relentless critiques. Each loss on the court felt like a personal failure, not just a scoreboard statistic, and Shawn found himself spiraling deeper into a fear of letting down the one person whose opinion mattered most.

As the matches piled up, so did the expectations. The thrill of the game was replaced by a cloud of anxiety that followed him home, into his dreams, and even into the early morning hours when he'd practice alone, hoping that if he just tried hard enough, he could erase the sting of disappointment. But with every missed serve and failed volley, the joy of tennis slipped further away, leaving only a hollow echo of what once was.

Eventually, Shawn made the difficult choice to step away from the sport. It was a cautionary moment, a bittersweet reflection of how the pressures of competition can snuff out the flame of talent and passion. In his silence, he let go of the racket but carried with him the lessons learned—not just about the game he loved but about the importance of finding worth beyond the scoreboard.

Recent studies have shed light on a troubling trend: young athletes who face intense pressure from their parents often struggle with feelings of inadequacy and a diminished sense of resilience (López, 2010). This connection underscores the profound impact that parental attitudes and behaviors can have on the mental well-being of aspiring young competitors, shaping not just their performance on the field but also their self-worth.

ASPIRATIONS AND EXPECTATIONS

Nurturing a child's aspirations while managing expectations is a dance that requires careful choreography. Take Micaela, for example. Her parents walked the fine line between encouragement and realism as they cheered her on in her track races. They wanted her to dream big, to set ambitious time goals that made her heart race with excitement. But alongside that thrill, they instilled in her a deeper understanding: it wasn't just about the finish line. It was about the thrill of every stride, the joy of running under the sun, and the lessons learned along the way.

Micaela thrived in this environment, her spirit buoyed by their support. With each race, she pushed herself, not out of fear or pressure, but from a genuine passion for the sport. She declared personal bests, not weighed down by sky-high expectations but instead lifted by the balance her parents cultivated. They had created a space where she felt free to chase her dreams, knowing that effort and enjoyment were the true markers of success.

Conversely, Nathaniel was fifteen and spent most of his afternoons on the basketball court, the scent of sweat mingling with the sound of sneakers squeaking against polished wood. It used to be his sanctuary, where the click of the ball and the swish of the net filled him with a sense of freedom. But lately, that magic had been overshadowed by the weight of expectations pressing down on him like a heavy backpack.

His parents had painted a picture of the future where he was a collegiate athlete, a dream they nurtured since he was little. They often drilled him about his performance, analyzing every shot and every game. "You need to work harder," they'd say, their faces a tapestry of hope and anxiety. What had once been a source of joy slowly transformed into an obligation, turning his love for the game into just another bar he had to reach.

As the pressure crescendoed, Nathaniel felt his own enthusiasm withering like a plant deprived of sunlight. The joy of the game was dwindling; burnout was creeping in. He was combining research in the back of his mind with real-life observations—kids who felt like they were valued only for their victories often lost sight of the why behind their pursuits.

Each dribble that echoed on the court became a reminder of the expectations he wasn't sure he could meet. The weight of his parents' dreams dulled his passion, and with each missed shot, the spark of excitement dimmed. In search of a way to reclaim his love for the sport, Nathaniel found himself retreating, pulling away from teammates, coaches, and even the game altogether, caught in a cycle he couldn't break.

Research indicates that when children believe their self-worth is tied exclusively to their achievements, they often experience a decline in motivation, ultimately paving the way for burnout and a sense of disconnection (Fletcher et al., 2013).

COMMUNICATION DYNAMICS

Effective communication forms the backbone of a supportive athletic environment. Where the roar of cheers and the crunch of grass underfoot reign supreme, effective communication stands as the unseen foundation of a nurturing team environment. Picture a parent crouched on the sidelines, eyes sparkling with encouragement, as they share a quick word of praise with their star player, their own child. It's in these moments of connection that motivation flourishes, igniting a passion for the game that goes beyond the scoreboard.

In the quiet hum of the car after practice, the familiar scent of sweat and grass lingered in the air as Megan settled into the backseat, her muscles still tingling from the evening's exertion. Her parents glanced at her in the rearview mirror, their expressions open and inviting.

"So, Meg, what was the highlight of today's practice?" her dad asked, his tone light yet genuinely curious.

Megan's face brightened. "I finally nailed that flip I've been working on for weeks!"

Her mom, catching a smile, chimed in. "That's amazing! What was it that made it click for you?"

As the car glided along the road, filled with the sounds of familiar music playing softly, the conversation flowed effortlessly. They talked not just about the drills and challenges, but also about the thrill of the game and what it meant for Megan personally. Underneath the casual banter, something deeper was taking root—the understanding that her journey in athletics mattered, that her voice was heard and valued.

These moments weren't just idle chit-chat. They were the threads weaving a tapestry of support that bolstered Megan's enthusiasm and ownership of her path as a young athlete. With each exchange, her passion only deepened, and the bond with her parents strengthened, embodying the foundation of a nurturing environment where dreams could flourish.

Active listening isn't just a skill; it's the heartbeat of a healthy parent-child relationship, especially in the world of sports. When parents pause to genuinely tune in to their child's thoughts, feelings, and dreams, those young athletes come alive with a sense of worth and connection. On the flip side, when parents impose their own agendas without inviting their child into the conversation, it not only creates a rift but often leads to rebellion and disengagement. Research, like that from Brackenridge in 2001, underscores this reality: open communication can elevate both satisfaction and performance in young athletes. It serves as a reminder that dialogue isn't just a tool; it's the foundation upon which trust and growth can flourish in the parent-athlete dynamic.

ROLE MODELING AND BEHAVIOR

Parents often stand as the most significant figures in shaping their children's perspectives on success, failure, and the very essence of physical activity. Take Doug, for instance—a dedicated recreational runner who faced his fair share of injuries. Each time he overcame these setbacks, he did so with unwavering perseverance and an encouraging spirit. His daughter, Lily, watched intently, absorbing not just the outcomes of his efforts, but the attitude he brought to each challenge.

For Lily, her father's approach became a guiding light in her own athletic journey. When she stumbled during races or faced defeats on the field, she didn't see these moments as the end of her dreams. Instead, they evolved into stepping stones. Doug taught her that resilience isn't just about bouncing back; it's about embracing every twist and turn, every fall and setback, as a vital part of her growth. With each race, Lily learned to navigate the highs and lows, internalizing the belief that every challenge was an opportunity, a chapter in her own unfolding story.

The reverse is also true. Claire often found herself in the shadow of her parents' unfulfilled dreams. Their nights were filled with wistful stories of glory days on the field—too many anecdotes that echoed with disappointment. Each sigh from her father and each furrowed brow from her mother felt like a weight pressing down on her, igniting a deep-seated obligation to transform their regrets into her triumphs.

With every practice, Claire could feel the anxiety pooling in her stomach, a tangible reflection of their expectations clashing with her own fears. She was torn between wanting to excel for her sake and the deep dread of disappointing them. The pressure loomed like a storm cloud, shrouding her achievements in doubt.

A study by Bangsbo et al. (2015) highlights how crucial positive role models are in raising resilient young athletes, yet all Claire had were the remnants of her parents' frustrations—a perspective she couldn't seem to shake. As much as she wanted to carve her own path in sports, it had become almost impossible to see beyond the weight of their unmet aspirations.

NAVIGATING COMPETITION

Supporting young athletes in competitive environments requires more than talent to foster success; it requires a nuanced approach from parents who navigate the delicate balance of encouragement and support. Within this competitive arena, thoughtful guidance can make all the difference in managing a young athlete's expectations and anxieties.

Take Abigail, for instance. As the regional swim meet approached, her parents made a conscious choice. They shifted the focus from the podium to the pool, reminding her of the joy that came with lap after lap, stroke after stroke. Instead of fixating on winning or losing, they talked about what it meant to immerse herself in the experience—creating a mantra of passion over the podium. Together, they integrated relaxation techniques into their evenings, practicing visualization exercises that helped calm her nerves.

Across town, Elaine encouraged her youngest son, Jacob, to take ownership of his journey in the athletics world. She watched as he flourished when given the freedom to select his events and set his own goals. Inspired by the newfound autonomy, he approached each competition not with dread, but with a sense of adventure, viewing every challenge as a canvas for growth.

But not all families navigate these waters so thoughtfully. Some parents, perhaps well-meaning, wrap their children in an embrace too tight, controlling every aspect of the competitive experience. Research paints a sobering picture; in such high-pressure environments, young athletes often develop anxiety that casts a shadow over their passion, leading to avoidance and a waning interest in their chosen sports.

In the end, the stories of Abigail and Jacob resonate far beyond the finish lines; they remind us that fostering joy and resilience in youth athletics is not just about training harder, but about nurturing a healthy mindset—a lesson that echoes long after the trophies are put away.

Parental influence in youth sports encompasses a spectrum of behaviors that significantly shape young athletes' experiences, attitudes, and futures. When parents adopt a supportive stance— cheering from the stands, offering encouragement, and celebrating small victories—the result is often an environment rich in enjoyment and resilience. Young athletes flourish, discovering not just skills in their sport but also a sense of self-worth and joy in the game.

However, the pressure some parents exert can create a stark contrast. Instead of a love for the sport, these young athletes may find themselves engulfed in stress and burnout, pushing them to disengage entirely. It's a painful cycle that many experience, where the love of the game dims under the weight of expectations.

The real magic happens when parents foster open communication and model positivity. When they prioritize their child's happiness over rigid performance goals, they set the stage for a healthier athletic journey. This nurturing approach doesn't just cultivate exceptional sports skills; it shapes young people into well-rounded individuals, equipped to face life's challenges beyond the field.

As these athletes navigate their journeys, the influence of their parents is ever-present, a constant that can either elevate their experience or diminish it. In the end, it's more than just about becoming skilled players; it's about nurturing a new generation that understands the importance of passion, resilience, and authentic joy in all they pursue.

MENTAL HEALTH AWARENESS IN YOUNG ATHLETES

In the charged atmosphere of youth sports, where trophies gleam and victory roars, the urgent pursuit of excellence frequently eclipses a vital, yet often overlooked, aspect: mental health. Each young athlete, whether sprinting down a track, defending a goal, or aiming for the perfect shot, contends with a multitude of pressures. These stressors weave into the fabric of their daily lives, tugging at their resolve and shaping their psychological landscape in profound ways. Amidst the cheers and the competition, the silent battles of anxiety, fear, and self-doubt unfold—struggles that deserve to be recognized and addressed.

UNDERSTANDING UNIQUE STRESSORS

Young athletes navigate a complex landscape of expectations that can weigh heavily on their mental well-being. The relentless push for victory, often ingrained in a culture that glorifies winning above all else, can ferment a storm of stress that leaves them feeling anxious and overwhelmed. As they strive to meet these demands, the joy of their sport can sometimes fade into the background, overshadowed by the fear of failure and the pressure to excel.

Consider the story of Alice: The sun dipped low over the soccer field, casting long shadows as Alice laced up her cleats. At fifteen, the weight of expectations pressed down on her like an oppressive summer heat. The thrill of the game was often eclipsed by the gnawing anxiety of maintaining her spot in the competitive club. Every whistle from the referee felt like a verdict, and each game was a tightrope walk between triumph and despair.

As the whistle blew and the game began, Alice's thoughts spiraled. She remembered the way her teammates shot her sideways glances whenever she made a mistake, voices echoing in her mind—"not good enough," "you'll let us down." It all felt too much. As the final whistle blew, she felt the familiar sting of tears welling up, a tight knot forming in her throat. How had a game that once brought her joy turned into a source of such pain?

Data confirmed her struggles weren't solitary. Research indicated that nearly 35% of young athletes like Alice faced similar pressures, dancing on the razor's edge of performance anxiety and burnout (Gould et al., 2019). But as she trudged off the field, the joyful chaos of her teammates celebrating the win felt distant, a world she could no longer reach. All that remained was the deafening silence of her own disappointment and the relentless question: was it worth it?

The relentless scroll of social media can feel like an endless loop of highlights—a carefully curated gallery of aspiring young athletes living their best lives. Each post gleams with triumph: a perfect game, a championship win, a physique sculpted to perfection. For many, the pressure to measure up to this polished imagery is suffocating. It's not uncommon for these athletes to find themselves grappling with feelings of inadequacy, wondering why their own successes feel muted in comparison. The more they scroll, the more isolated they become, trapped in a cycle of comparison that has little to do with the reality of their own journeys. In the dim light of their rooms, with screens aglow, the weight of these expectations hangs heavy, turning what should be a passion into a source of anxiety.

In the glow of her phone, Amy scrolled through countless posts, each one a parade of flawless smiles and triumphant achievements. Her fellow athletes, bathed in golden sunlight, shared their victories and milestones, meticulously curated to portray lives brimming with success. But for Amy, the constant comparisons felt like weights being added to her chest, gradually suffocating the joy she once found on the track.

The once-innocent excitement of sharing her training sessions had morphed into an obsession with likes and comments, each notification igniting a fleeting spark of happiness that quickly fizzled to nothing. Anxiety tightened its grip, an unwelcome companion that whispered doubts and insecurities, drowning out the thrill of racing towards her goals. It was as if the sport she loved became a stage for others, while she played a role she no longer recognized.

Surveys suggested that athletes like her were grappling with similar shadows. The pressure of social media was palpable, suffusing their lives with an overwhelming sense of inadequacy and isolation (Purdy et al., 2021). As Amy looked around, an invisible curtain seemed to separate her from the very world she once felt connected to, leaving her longing for a time when running was simply about the wind in her hair and the freedom underfoot.

SIGNS AND SYMPTOMS

Spotting the early signs of mental health challenges in young athletes is crucial for ensuring their well-being. These indicators can manifest in different ways, including:

Changes in Mood: Athletes can often experience a shift in their emotional landscape, leading to irritability or sadness that distances them from their loved ones. Sam, once the shimmering star of the swim team, began to fade into the shadows after a string of disappointing races. His enthusiasm, once as vibrant as the blue waters he swam through, gave way to deep-seated despair, pushing friends and teammates away as he retreated into himself.

Withdrawal from Social Activities: A noticeable drop in social engagement can be a warning sign of internal struggles. Emily, whose feet once flew with the grace of a gazelle on the track, slowly started backing away from team events and training sessions. The vibrant conversations and laughter that filled the air during practice faded, leaving her feeling more like a ghost haunting the edges of her own life—isolating herself in a protective shell as the weight of her mental health pressed down on her.

Decline in Performance: A sudden slump in performance often points to underlying challenges that run deeper than the athletes' physical abilities. Studies indicate that athletes grappling with mental health issues frequently find their focus and motivation slipping away, dramatically impacting their capacity to compete. For instance, when the scoreboard started reflecting her struggles, Emily felt the flicker of doubt grow into a roaring flame—every lost race felt like a personal failure, unraveling the confidence she had fought so hard to build.

Changes in Sleep or Eating Patterns: Disruptions in sleep or eating habits can reveal the toll of mental conflicts on an athlete's well-being. Nathan, a once-vibrant basketball player, started to experience restless nights filled with anxiety as game days approached. Desperate to quell the tension building inside him, he turned to food—a temporary solace that left him feeling bloated and regretful. Each bite was a way to cope with the soaring expectations, but the relief it brought was fleeting, overshadowed by the stress that had snuck into his life like an unwelcome guest.

CREATING A SUPPORTIVE ENVIRONMENT

Creating an environment that nurtures emotional wellness in young athletes isn't just a good idea—it's essential. It calls for thoughtful strategies we can adopt as parents and coaches. Here's how you can cultivate that supportive space:

Embrace Open Communication: It's important to foster a culture where athletes feel safe sharing their thoughts and feelings. Encourage them to express their fears, excitement, and even their disappointments, without the looming shadow of judgment. Let them know their voices matter.

Practice Validation: When an athlete is grappling with a tough game or a disappointing loss, acknowledging their emotions can make a world of difference. Tell them it's perfectly okay to have off days—what matters is how they pick themselves back up afterward.

Encourage Balance: Remind young athletes that life is more than just the next game or competition. Help them carve out time for hobbies, friendships, and adventures outside of their sport. This balance can prevent the weight of athletic expectations from becoming all-consuming.

Focus on Skill Development: Equip athletes with coping mechanisms like mindfulness and relaxation techniques. These skills serve as vital tools that can empower them to navigate the pressures of competition with resilience.

The journey of sports should be one of growth, not just in skills but in emotional strength too. By integrating these strategies into our daily interactions, we help lay a foundation for a healthier, more supportive experience for every young athlete.

PROMOTING EDUCATION AND AWARENESS

In the heat of competition, where the roaring crowd and flashing lights often drown out inner struggles, mental health education must find its place in the heart of sports programs. It's essential to weave discussions about mental wellbeing into the fabric of athletic training, opening up conversations that are just as vital as physical conditioning.

Imagine workshops conducted not just in stuffy meeting rooms, but on the field, where athletes, coaches, and families can come together, share stories, and absorb critical information about mental health. Here, knowledge transforms into power—teaching them how to recognize the subtle signs of emotional distress and arming them with effective strategies to reach out and support one another.

Just like perfecting a free throw or honing a sprint, understanding mental health requires practice and dedication. By integrating these tools into the training regimen, we create a culture where seeking help is seen not as a sign of weakness but as a courageous step toward personal growth. In this new arena, every player knows they're not just a part of a team on the field, but a community committed to looking out for one another, both in triumph and in hardship.

For example, a school sports program in California implemented a "Mental Health Matters" workshop for all athletes, resulting in increased awareness and the establishment of peer support groups (Johnson et al., 2023).

Teaching athletes that mental health challenges are a common part of their experience helps remove the stigma surrounding them and encourages open discussions about seeking help. By cultivating an educational atmosphere focused on mental health within the sports community, we empower young athletes to understand their own struggles and advocate for their well-being, just as they would for their physical training. This shift not only fosters resilience but also creates a supportive environment where everyone feels comfortable sharing their experiences and seeking assistance when needed.

In the world of young athletes, the path to success is seldom a smooth one. Beyond the sweat and the triumphs on the field lies a more complex and often overlooked battle—one that takes place within the mind. It's a reality that demands our attention: mental health challenges affect not just how athletes play, but how they grow as individuals.

To truly support our young stars, we must cultivate awareness around these issues, taking the time to recognize the subtle signs of distress that might otherwise go unnoticed. Creating environments that uplift and nurture is essential, as this support plays a crucial role in allowing them to flourish—not just as competitors, but as well-rounded individuals.

The pressure is immense, driven by the pursuit of trophies and applause, but the stakes reach far beyond the podium. We owe it to our future generations to prioritize their holistic well-being, ensuring they feel valued and understood. Addressing mental health isn't a one-time conversation; it requires ongoing dedication from all corners of youth sports—coaches, parents, teammates, and communities alike.

Together, we can weave a fabric of support that empowers these young athletes to navigate their journeys, ultimately helping them to thrive in competition and in life.

BALANCING SPORTS, EDUCATION, AND SOCIAL LIFE

In the lives of young athletes, the quest for greatness on the field often parallels the heavy weight of academics and the innate longing for social connection. Balancing these competing demands can feel like a high-wire act, where every decision is a carefully choreographed move, each choice a potential misstep that threatens to send them tumbling. This chapter delves into the myriad challenges these young competitors face as they strive to juggle their varied responsibilities. We'll uncover the rewards of finding that vital equilibrium, explore practical strategies for managing their time more effectively, and highlight the essential role of their support systems. We'll also discuss the subtle yet unmistakable signs of burnout and emphasize the critical need for social ties that keep them grounded amid the chaos of their ambitious lives.

THE JUGGLING ACT

Meet Mina, a 16-year-old soccer prodigy and honor roll student whose life is a whirlwind of drills and deadlines. Each day unfolds with relentless intensity: the piercing whistle of the coach signaling the start of another practice, followed by the late-night scramble to finish her homework under the dim glow of a desk lamp. In the beginning, her schedule is filled with the excitement of games, the triumph of personal bests, and the satisfaction of good grades. Mina thrives on this chaos, believing she can conquer the world if only she keeps running just a little faster.

But as the high school soccer season drags on, Mina's world starts to tilt. The thrill of scoring goals is overshadowed by a creeping fatigue that settles over her like a thick fog. Each early morning run feels heavier, each textbook more daunting. The weight of expectations—both from herself and others—threatens to pull her down.

Mina isn't alone in this struggle. A study by Balaguer et al. (2017) highlights a reality that resonates far beyond her small soccer team: young athletes often feel a unique strain that eclipses that of their non-athletic peers. The interplay of practices, competitions, homework, and a semblance of social life creates a juggling act that seems more precarious by the day. With every calculated move, Mina teeters on a high wire stretched above her aspirations, trying to find balance without losing herself in the fall. As the season deepens, the question weighs heavily on her mind: how long can she keep this up before something—herself, her passion—snaps?

THE BENEFITS OF BALANCE

Finding balance is more than just a numbers game; it's a lifeline that can transform the everyday lives of young athletes. Studies, like those from Gould and his colleagues in 2016, reveal that striking a healthy equilibrium between sports, schoolwork, and social activities can significantly boost performance across the board. When these young athletes learn to juggle their responsibilities effectively, they often find themselves grappling with less stress and anxiety. This newfound control nurtures their emotional health and builds resilience, equipping them to tackle challenges on and off the field.

Consider

Forest, a 17-year-old basketball player, learned early on that life was a delicate equation. While the court beckoned with its exhilarating intensity, he refused to let it overshadow everything else. The thrill of a three-pointer was exhilarating, but so was the laughter shared with friends over late-night study sessions or the quiet satisfaction that came from acing a difficult exam.

By carving out time for both academics and social connections, he began to notice a shift in his game. The focus he cultivated in the classroom translated to a newfound clarity on the hardwood. The rhythm of his life felt more harmonious—a balance that fueled his aspirations and kept the stress of competition at bay.

Forest wasn't alone in his realization. Research echoed his experience; countless studies indicated that athletes who pursued diverse interests often found deeper satisfaction and faced fewer burnouts. As he savored the camaraderie of team drills and the thrill of the game, it was this balance that transformed him, shaping him not just as a player, but as a person navigating the complexities of youth.

TIME MANAGEMENT STRATEGIES

In the bustling life of a young athlete, where the pressures of competition and academics intersect, finding balance is not just a goal; it's a necessity. The world outside is a whirlwind of training schedules, classes, and social commitments, all vying for attention. Here's how young athletes can navigate this juggling act with grace and efficiency.

Craft a Weekly Plan: Think of a weekly schedule not as a rigid structure, but as a canvas for clarity. By plotting out training sessions, classes, study periods, and even social outings, athletes can see their commitments laid out in front of them. It's like drawing a map for the week—every commitment given its rightful place, allowing for a clearer path forward.

Rank Your Responsibilities: Imagine a priority matrix where tasks are sorted by urgency and importance. High-priority assignments should take center stage. If Lucas has a chemistry test looming, he can tackle those study sessions first, ensuring he dedicates enough time to grasp the material without the last-minute stress.

Establish Attainable Goals: When faced with a daunting mountain of objectives, breaking it down into smaller, digestible tasks can be a game changer. Take Sarah, for instance, who wants to excel in her history class. By committing to reading a chapter a day rather than cramming the night before, she transforms a potentially overwhelming task into a routine that fits seamlessly into her life.

Embrace Adaptability: Life, with all its unpredictability, often disrupts even the best-laid plans. That's why it's wise to weave a little flexibility into the schedule. Allowing for some buffer time around activities means there's space to breathe and make adjustments when life throws a curveball.

Minimize Interruptions: In the midst of study sessions or intense training, distractions can derail progress. By turning off notifications or creating a focused environment, athletes can cultivate a mindset that fosters productivity. It's about carving out that sacred time, where attention is fully devoted to the task at hand.

By implementing these strategies, young athletes can find not just balance, but the confidence to thrive in all areas of their lives, mastering the art of time management one day at a time.

THE ROLE OF SUPPORT SYSTEMS

Where the pressures of competition and personal growth collide, having a solid support system can mean the difference between success and struggle. Coaches, with their keen insights and relentless dedication, become more than just instructors; they are beacons of guidance, illuminating the often-turbulent path ahead. Mentors step in with invaluable experiences, sharing hard-won wisdom that resonates deeply. Family members stand as unwavering pillars, offering encouragement and a shoulder to lean on when the weight of expectations feels too heavy. Friends, too, contribute to this intricate tapestry of support, bringing laughter and camaraderie that lighten the burdens young athletes carry. In this delicate balance of ambition and vulnerability, it's the network of people surrounding them that helps these athletes navigate the complexities of their lives, forging resilience and a sense of belonging amidst the challenges they face.

Dhriti stood at the edge of the track, her heart pounding as the sun dipped below the horizon, casting long shadows across the field. Her coach, a seasoned veteran with a calm demeanor, had urged her to speak up whenever the weight of competition felt too heavy. "Voice it out, Dhriti," he'd said, "Don't let it fester inside."

That advice had become a lifeline for her. Whenever anxiety gripped her, she learned to articulate her worries—whether it was a nagging fear of letting her teammates down or the pressure of chasing personal records. This dialogue with her coach wasn't just a formality; it was a transformation. It allowed them to tweak her training schedule, packing in rest days without sacrificing the grind needed for peak performance.

Research echoed this small but meaningful change; studies suggested that supportive relationships could bolster the mental resilience of young athletes, helping them navigate the turbulent waters of competition. For Dhriti, these adjustments made all the difference. With the burden of her fears lightened, she found herself not just racing against her opponents but also discovering a newfound balance within herself.

In the tight-knit fabric of their lives, the committee members, teammates, and friends formed a constellation of support. Take Daniel, for instance. When the pressures of the basketball season caused his grades to slip like a wayward ball bouncing off the rim, his study group sprang into action. They gathered around him, textbooks and notes spread like a patchwork quilt, each person contributing their strengths. It was more than just academics; it was a powerful reminder of how forming connections and leaning on one another not only shared the burden but stitched their community closer together, reinforcing a sense of accountability and shared purpose.

RECOGNIZING SIGNS OF BURNOUT

Young athletes, like everyone else, can fall prey to burnout—a condition marked by a deep weariness, both in body and spirit, that leaves them feeling drained and less fulfilled. It creeps in quietly, often manifesting as constant exhaustion, a short temper, and a waning interest in what once brought them joy. Their usual excitement for practice dims, performance suffers, and they may find themselves withdrawing from friends and teammates, lost in a haze of discontent (Raedeke & Smith, 2001).

Recognizing these signs is crucial for timely intervention. Phoebe sat on the edge of her bed, staring blankly at the sneakers she had tossed haphazardly into the corner. Each pair represented a different chapter of her life, filled with hopes and dreams that now felt heavy, almost oppressive. She sank deeper into her thoughts, the weight of stress and exhaustion pressing down on her like a thick blanket. If only she had recognized the signs sooner—the sleepless nights, the growing impatience with her friends, the gnawing dread before every practice. Maybe she could have found the words to express how overwhelmed she felt, to reach out for help before everything spiraled out of control.

The wise voices in her head echoed reminders she had previously scoffed at. She pictured those scheduled rest periods her coach had suggested, days carved out for nothing but basking in quiet stillness. Young athletes often scoff at rest, but what they fail to understand is that the body and mind need that space to recuperate and revitalize. Phoebe also thought about mindfulness practices—simple things like meditation or yoga that felt far removed from the intense competition she loved. Yet, when she looked in the mirror, she didn't recognize the girl staring back at her anymore. She needed to reconnect, to breathe and reflect, to rediscover the joy and passion that once fueled her every stride on the track.

Now, standing at a crossroads, Phoebe resolved to listen to her own voice. She began to imagine a future where she didn't race against her own needs, where scheduled rest wasn't a luxury, but a strategy. A life where mindfulness was a tool, not just a buzzword —an anchor that could help ground her in moments of chaos. And perhaps, just perhaps, she could reclaim her rhythm before the music faded away entirely.

BALANCING SOCIAL LIFE

In the whirlwind of practices, competitions, and relentless studying, young athletes often find themselves caught in a relentless tide of expectations. The drive to excel in sports and academics can become all-consuming, leading them to neglect a crucial aspect of their lives: social connections. Yet, it's in those moments spent with friends, sharing laughter and stories, that true enrichment occurs. Friendships aren't just a welcome distraction from the rigors of training and homework—they are vital sources of emotional support that help weather the storms of stress and competition.

The research underscores this importance, revealing a strong link between social engagement and academic achievement. When students cultivate relationships, they often find improved performance in the classroom, suggesting that the bonds they forge off the field can give them the strength to excel in their pursuits. It's a reminder that while the scoreboard may capture the thrill of victory, it's the laughter and camaraderie shared with friends that truly make the journey worthwhile.

For Daniel, the game didn't define him entirely. While his days were consumed by the rhythm of basketball—dribbling, shooting, and the unrelenting grind of practice—he found solace in moments spent with friends who shared little more than his laugh and love for life. Their evening hangouts, filled with laughter and the glow of late-night movie marathons, became a refuge after the pressure of another demanding week on the court.

It was during those easy, conversation-filled nights that Daniel discovered a different kind of connection—one not bound by the sport but by a shared sense of humor, mutual dreams, and the occasional absurdity of teenage life. It was in these interactions that he unearthed the richness of friendship beyond competition. He learned that while basketball might illuminate his path, it was these ordinary gatherings that anchored him, allowing him to breathe and recharge away from the bright lights and relentless expectations of the game.

As this chapter illustrates, the delicate art of balancing sports, education, and social life is an ongoing journey for young athletes. Through the lens of effective time management, we see how essential it is for these young competitors to carve out moments for study, practice, and relaxation. Building strong support networks—friends, family, and coaches who understand the balancing act—becomes a lifeline when challenges mount. Recognizing the signs of burnout is crucial; it quietly creeps in and can derail even the most dedicated athletes. By also making space for social connections, they enrich not only their game but their overall experience as they prepare to navigate the complexities of life beyond the field or court. This blend of dedication, awareness, and support lays the groundwork for them to flourish, both as athletes and as individuals equipped to face whatever comes their way.

CULTIVATING A POSITIVE ATHLETIC MINDSET

In the realm of sports, it's easy to get swept up in the glimmer of athletic prowess: the breathtaking speed of a sprinter, the raw power of a lineman, the graceful agility of a gymnast. These physical traits typically steal the spotlight, becoming the benchmarks by which we measure greatness. Yet, beneath the surface of every successful athlete lies an equally vital dimension—one that rarely gets the same attention. This dimension is the psychological makeup of the athlete, a complex web of emotions, thoughts, and beliefs that can be either a powerful ally or a formidable foe.

In this chapter, we delve into the heart of what makes champions, examining the strategies that can nurture a resilient mindset in young athletes. It's about more than just training the body; it's about equipping the mind with the tools to flourish—not just on the field, but in life. From fostering self-confidence to embracing failure as a stepping stone to success, we'll explore the methods that can help these young athletes thrive in their sports journey, turning challenges into opportunities and setbacks into growth. Join us as we uncover the essential psychological components that are just as vital as physical strength—elements that, when developed, can lead to lasting success both in sports and beyond.

UNDERSTANDING GROWTH MINDSET

The concept of a growth mindset looms large, shaping not just the trajectory of budding athletes but the very fabric of their experiences. Imagine a young runner, the morning sun illuminating the track as she stretches, her breath steady and her heart racing—not merely from the thrill of competition, but from the palpable understanding that every drop of sweat is a step towards her potential. This powerful notion, articulated by psychologist Carol Dweck, conveys that talent and intelligence are not fixed attributes, but fluid qualities crafted through perseverance and effort.

Contrast this with a young player who believes that talent is a gift —something bestowed at birth rather than nurtured through grit and practice. For him, each misstep feels like a verdict, every failure an unchangeable truth. The stakes of this mindset are high; it shackles his growth and dims the spark of possibility.

In the world of young athletes, embracing a growth mindset is akin to unlocking a treasure chest of continuous learning and improvement. Each setback transforms into an opportunity to learn, and every small triumph becomes a building block toward mastery. It's a journey where mistakes are not failures but vital lessons, where resilience becomes as significant as speed, and where the spirit of competition is matched only by the commitment to becoming better. This is the landscape shaped by a growth mindset, a landscape where the horizon is ever-expanding, inviting young athletes to run, learn, and evolve.

Consider the story of Olivia, a twelve-year-old soccer player.

Just a season prior, the mere thought of dribbling a soccer ball left her fraught with anxiety. The ball seemed to have a mind of its own, dancing away from her feet with an almost mocking glee. Each failed attempt to pass or shoot felt like a concrete weight on her chest, instilling a disheartening belief: she simply wasn't cut out for this sport.

But everything began to change during a particularly dreary practice. Coach Thompson, a wiry figure with a ponytail and an infectious enthusiasm, gathered the girls around him. "You know," he began, his eyes twinkling, "the greatest players aren't those who never stumble; they're the ones who see every stumble as a step forward." In that moment, he introduced them to the concept of a growth mindset—a simple yet profound idea that resonated deeply with Olivia.

With newfound resolve, she started to reshape her thoughts. Instead of cringing at her mistakes, she began to whisper a mantra to herself: "Every mistake is just a chance to improve." It wasn't easy. Every practice still felt like a battle, and there were days when the ball's defiance felt absolute. Yet, with each session that passed, she learned to embrace the stumbles, to laugh at the missteps, and to celebrate the small victories. Her dribbling improved, her passing became sharper, and with each drop of sweat, Olivia felt a transformation brewing not just in her skills, but within her very essence.

In her heart, a fire ignited—a passion for the game that made the setbacks pale in comparison to the thrill of progress. She practiced relentlessly, often staying late with her best friend, challenging each other to push past their limits. As weeks melted into a season, Olivia evolved from the uncertain player of the past into a dazzling force on the field, her confidence swelling with each game.

When it came time for the championship match, Olivia channeled all her hard work, all her newfound belief, into every stride she took. The final minutes ticked away, and with the score knotted, it seemed destiny had woven a tale just for her. The ball sailed toward her, and without a second thought, she executed a perfect pass, setting up the winning goal. Cheers erupted around her as her teammates enveloped her in a jubilant embrace.

In that moment, Olivia realized the truth: this victory was so much more than the championship trophy they would hoist later. It was a testament to her journey—a journey fueled by resilience and a shift in how she viewed herself. She had learned that talent might provide a head start, but true success blooms from the understanding that growth knows no bounds. And as she basked in the glory of the moment, she understood that the real trophy was the mindset she carried away from the field—a mindset that could spark new adventures beyond soccer's green expanse.

The difference between reaching their potential and falling short often hinges on their mindset. Research reveals that those who embrace a growth mindset—believing that abilities can be developed through hard work and dedication—tend to find themselves more motivated and resilient. This unwavering belief can translate to higher performance, as demonstrated by the work of Yeager and Dweck in 2012. For emerging athletes, fostering this mindset is not just about improving their game; it serves as a vital foundation for their overall development as both competitors and individuals. The journey is not merely a race toward victory, but a path filled with lessons in perseverance and self-discovery.

POSITIVE SELF-TALK

Self-talk plays a vital role in an athlete's mindset and performance, shaping the way they see themselves and approach their sport. The dialogue that loops through their minds can be a powerful force, influencing not just their feelings but also their actions on the field or court. For young athletes, who are still finding their footing, it's all too easy to fall into the trap of negative thinking. These unwelcome thoughts can shake their confidence and throw off their game. It's essential for them to identify when their mind is veering into dark territory and to actively swap those harmful messages for affirmations and positive self-talk. By doing so, they can build a resilient mindset that propels them forward, turning potential setbacks into stepping stones for growth.

Consider the experience of Sebastian, who felt the familiar flutter of anxiety in his stomach as he laced up his sneakers in the dimly lit locker room. It was game day, and despite the excitement of playing, he couldn't shake the persistent voice in his head whispering, "You're going to fail." Each time he stepped onto the court, that voice grew louder, drowning out the cheers of his teammates and the rhythm of the bouncing ball.

But today was different. Coach Ramirez had noticed Sebastian's struggle. He had pulled him aside during practice, his brow furrowed with concern. "Listen, Seb," he had said, his tone firm yet encouraging. "You need to change that inner dialogue. Instead of worrying about what might go wrong, focus on what you can do right."

Sebastian thought back to that moment as he wiped the sweat from his brow, the sound of sneakers squeaking against polished wood echoing in his ears. Taking a deep breath, he remembered the words the coach had shared. "I am prepared," he murmured under his breath, forcing the phrase to settle in his mind. The fear still hovered, but he began to recognize it as just a part of the game, not the entirety of it.

As he jogged onto the court, the cheers from the crowd started to feel less daunting. With each dribble, he reminded himself, "I will give my best effort." The mantra became his shield, helping him push through the jitters. He could hear the encouragement from his teammates, feel the weight of the ball in his hands, and suddenly, it wasn't just about winning or losing — it was about enjoying the game he loved.

With every shot, every play, and each moment spent on the court, Sebastian felt a shift. The anxiety didn't disappear completely; instead, it transformed into a charged energy, fueling him to move with finesse and confidence. He was no longer trapped in the cage of fear; he was free to embrace the joy of the game, discovering that it was about more than just the final score. It was a celebration of effort, teamwork, and the love of basketball that had brought him to this moment.

Research has shown that positive self-talk can significantly boost confidence and performance, acting as a powerful ally in building mental resilience and focus among athletes (Thelwell, 2013). For young athletes, having a set of affirmations ready to recite before games can be transformative. These simple mantras not only help to mold their mindset but also prepare them to tackle challenges head-on. By weaving these affirmations into their pre-game routine, they set themselves up for success, fostering a stronger, more determined approach to competition.

MINDFULNESS AND FOCUS

In the world of competitive sports, where every heartbeat feels like a countdown and the stakes hang heavy in the air, the ability to focus sharply and manage stress becomes a game-changer. For young athletes standing on the brink of their dreams, the pressure can be immense. Here, mindfulness practices emerge as a lifeline, offering strategies that go beyond mere physical training.

Imagine a swimmer at the edge of the pool, the noise of cheering fans fading as they close their eyes. Deep breathing becomes their anchor, each inhale a wave, each exhale a ripple, carrying away the doubt that once held them. They visualize the race ahead, feeling the water gliding past them, their strokes precise and fluid. In that moment, they are not just preparing for competition; they are mastering the art of presence, training their minds to stand strong against the turbulent tide of anxiety that often threatens to engulf them.

As young athletes learn to harness these techniques—be it through mindful meditation before a game or silent moments of reflection during practice—they find a reservoir of calm amid chaos. This quiet confidence doesn't just enhance their ability to concentrate; it transforms their approach to the game altogether, allowing them to play with a clarity that elevates their performance and deepens their love for the sport.

The countdown had begun for Anika, a fifteen-year-old gymnast, stood on the precipice of a dream—her first national competition. As the countdown began, a familiar knot of anxiety twisted in her stomach. The spotlight felt both exhilarating and suffocating, a whirlwind of hopes and fears crashing together.

Her coach noticed the tension etched on her brow and introduced her to the calming world of mindfulness meditation. At first, it felt strange to close her eyes and focus solely on her breath while the world buzzed with excitement around her. But with each session, Anika found solace in the gentle rhythm of inhaling and exhaling, grounding herself amid the chaos.

Visualization became her secret weapon. In her mind's eye, she pictured herself soaring through the air, executing each routine with grace—each twist and turn a brushstroke on a canvas only she could see. Slowly, the doubt began to fade, replaced by a growing confidence that her body was capable of incredible things.

When the day of the competition finally arrived, Anika stood backstage, her heart racing, but she dug deep into her newfound toolkit. Whispering encouraging words to herself like a quiet mantra, she inhaled deeply, feeling the oxygen fill her lungs and push out the fear.

As she stepped out onto the mat, everything fell silent except for the rhythmic thump of her heartbeat. With each movement, a newfound clarity washed over her. The routine she had practiced for countless hours flowed seamlessly, a dance of determination and poise.

When the final landing echoed through the arena, Anika felt more than relief; she felt triumph. It was, without a doubt, her best performance yet, not just because of the routines she executed but because she conquered the anxiety that came with them. In that moment, the pressures of competition melted away, and all that remained was the sheer joy of doing what she loved.

The research underscores the benefits of mindfulness in athletics, suggesting it sharpens focus, alleviates anxiety, and fosters a deeper enjoyment of the sport (Kreitzer et al., 2018). For young athletes grappling with the emotional rollercoaster of competition, integrating mindfulness practices can prove to be an invaluable resource, helping them find balance amid the highs and lows of their experiences.

REGULAR REFLECTION AND GROWTH EVALUATION

To build a strong and positive athletic mindset, young athletes need to make reflection and self-evaluation a regular part of their routine. By taking time to assess their progress, celebrate their achievements, and set fresh intentions, they come to grasp that growth is an ongoing journey, not just a destination. Rather than getting caught up in the final scores or outcomes, they can focus on how they performed in relation to their personal goals and the strides they've made along the way. This shift in perspective helps them appreciate the process and fuels their passion for improvement.

Mason, a sixteen-year-old with dreams of tennis stardom, discovered the transformative art of reflection thanks to his coach's end-of-week ritual. Each Friday, they would sit down, a worn notebook lying open between them, its pages filled with scores and scribbled notes from past matches. It was here that Mason learned to dissect his performance—not just the errors that echoed in his mind, but the triumphs too, however small.

During these sessions, Mason would sift through moments of brilliance alongside lapses in focus. His coach would guide him through the highlights—the time he nailed that backhand winner down the line, the way he outmaneuvered his opponent during a crucial rally. It wasn't just about tallying wins and losses; it was about understanding the game itself and unearthing the lessons hidden beneath the surface.

He would jot down what worked and what didn't, formulating specific goals with a clarity that fueled his determination for the days ahead. This ritual, far from being a chore, became a source of motivation, igniting a passion for growth that resonated deep within him. With each reflection, Mason learned to appreciate not just the victories but the journey itself, finding inspiration in the process of improvement—a reminder that even in the face of setbacks, there was always a new challenge waiting to be tackled.

Research suggests that when athletes engage in reflective practices, they experience a significant boost in their learning and personal growth, a notion supported by the work of Gould and Udry in 1994. This method nurtures a culture of ongoing self-improvement, urging athletes not just to participate in their sport but to actively shape their development journey, embracing each experience as a crucial leap towards their goals.

In the world of young athletes, where dreams collide with dedication, cultivating a positive athletic mindset becomes a powerful tool for growth. It's not just about the plays made on the field or the races run on the track; it's about the belief that pulses in their hearts, the resilience that fuels their training, and the self-talk that crafts their inner dialogue.

Through the lens of mindfulness and reflection, these young dreamers learn to navigate the ups and downs of competition with grace. They discover that their talents are not set in stone but can evolve beautifully through hard work and a relentless spirit. Coaches, parents, and mentors hold a vital role in this transformative journey, guiding these athletes to embrace psychological strategies that extend far beyond their sport.

With this support, young athletes don't just improve their game; they build character. They learn that every setback is an opportunity for growth, and that every success is a stepping stone towards further achievement. In nurturing these strengths, we equip them not only for victories on the field but for the challenges that life will inevitably throw their way. In cultivating this mindset, we create not just competitors, but resilient individuals ready to tackle whatever comes next.

CONCLUSION

In wrapping up our conversation about young athletes, it's clear that developmental psychology gives us a unique and insightful way to comprehend their complex journeys. When we take a closer look at their cognitive, emotional, social, and physical growth, we see just how vital it is to approach each athlete as an individual, one who needs more than just skill-building. It's about nurturing their overall well-being, too.

As these young athletes grow, their motivations and performances shift. In those early years, the sheer joy of play and exploration can ignite a lifelong passion for sports. But then comes the tricky terrain of adolescence, a time that demands extra emotional support from both coaches and parents. This is where the right guidance can make all the difference.

Coaches and parents have the incredible opportunity to create environments where encouragement and celebration take precedence over sheer competition. It's in the camaraderie of teammates that young athletes learn valuable life lessons, discovering the strength that comes from collaboration and friendship. Recognizing their developmental needs—like how to manage emotions and build cognitive skills—is essential for fostering resilience, ensuring that the pressure to perform doesn't overshadow the simple pleasures of playing the game.

Finding a balance between competition and enjoyment is crucial, especially in a culture that tends to push for early specialization. As these young athletes embark on their personal journeys, they begin to cultivate motivation that stems from passion, not just from seeking approval. This shift helps them appreciate the growth process itself, deepening their connection to the sport.

Ultimately, the stories woven through the lives of young athletes —filled with struggles and achievements—underscore the powerful relationship between developmental psychology and the world of athletics. By focusing on their holistic development, we're not just preparing them for success on the field; we're equipping them for a fulfilling life beyond it. This way, they can emerge from their athletic experiences as well-rounded individuals, ready to take on the various challenges life throws their way with confidence and resilience.

ABOUT THE AUTHOR

Rapolas Janonis, commonly referred to as Coach Rap, is an author with an extensive background in competitive swimming and coaching. His most recent publication encapsulates the valuable insights he has acquired over years of commitment to the holistic development of athletes. Born in Lithuania during the Soviet Union era, Rap commenced his swimming journey in childhood and has had the honor of representing his country on the international stage.

Coach Rap's dedication to the sport of swimming led him to the United States, where he pursued collegiate-level competition and further developed his profound appreciation for aquatic disciplines. Holding a master's degree in kinesiology, he has spent more than two decades studying complexities of specificity and sports psychology, which has influenced his distinctive coaching philosophy centered on the mind-body connection.

BIBLIOGRAPHY

Brewer, B. W. (1993). *Self-identity and the role of sport.* In J. M. Williams (Ed.), Applied Sport Psychology: Personal Growth to Peak Performance. McGraw Hill.

Ericsson, K. A., Krampe, R. T., & Tesch-Römer, C. (1993). *The role of deliberate practice in the acquisition of expert performance.* Psychological Review, 100(3), 363-406.

Fletcher, D., & Sarkar, M. (2012). *A grounded theory of psychological resilience in Olympic champions.* Psychology of Sport and Exercise, 13(5), 669-678.

Gould, D., & Udry, E. (1994). *Psychological skills for enhancing performance: A review.* Sports Psychologist, 8(3), 240-256.

Helsen, W. F., & Starkes, J. L. (1999). A multidimensional approach to skill acquisition in sport. In J. L. Starkes & K. A. Ericsson (Eds.), *Expert Performance in Sports: Recent Advances in Research on Sport Expertise.* Human Kinetics.

Couts, K. (2019). How Enjoyment Impacts Youth Sports Participation. *Journal of Sports Psychology,* 32(1), 34-50.

Dweck, C. S. (2006). *Mindset: The New Psychology of Success.* Random House.

Erikson, E. H. (1968). *Identity: Youth and Crisis.* W.W. Norton & Company.

Fredricks, J. A., & Eccles, J. S. (2004). Pa*rental Involvement in Academic Activities: The Role of Parents' and Adolescents' Perceptions.* Psychology in the Schools, 41(6), 727-740.

Holt, N. L., & Dunn, J. G. H. (2004). Toward a Model of Youth Sport Participation. *Journal of Sport Psychology in Action,* 1(3), 121-132.

López, J. F., et al. (2019). *Early Specialization and Burnout in Young Athletes: An Affective Neuroscience Perspective.* International Journal of Sports Science & Coaching, 14(4), 418-427.

Piaget, J. (1952). *The Origins of Intelligence in Children.* International Universities Press.

Smith, R. E., et al. (2012). *Team Dynamics and Young Athletes: A Psychological Perspective.* In the annual review of sports science, 1, 235-257.

Bandura, A. (1977). *Self-efficacy: Toward a unifying theory of behavioral change.* Psychological Review, 84(2), 191-215.

Bandura, A. (1986). The explanatory and predictive scope of self-efficacy theory. *Journal of Social and Clinical Psychology,* 4(3), 359-373.

Bandura, A. (1997). *Self-efficacy: The exercise of control.* New York: W.H. Freeman.

Moritz, S.E., Feltz, D.L., Fahrbach, K.R., & Mack, D.E. (2000). The influence of self-efficacy on performance. *Journal of Sport and Exercise Psychology,* 22(2), 298-316.

Schunk, D.H. (2003). Self-efficacy for reading and writing: Influence of modeling, goal setting, and self-evaluation. *Reading and Writing Quarterly*, 19(2), 159-172.

Smith, R.E., Smoll, F.L., & Cumming, S.P. (2017). Effects of a coach training program on children's self-esteem and team cohesion. *International Journal of Sports Science & Coaching*, 12(2), 220-230.

Bailey, R., & Morley, D. (2011). *Sport and Exercise Science*. London: Routledge.

Cumming, J., & Hall, C. (2002). Imagery, confidence and anxiety in sport. *Journal of Sports Sciences*, 20(6), 541-553.

Dweck, C. S. (2006). *Mindset: The New Psychology of Success*. New York: Ballantine Books.

Gould, D., & Udry, E. (1994). *Psychological Skills for Enhancing Performance: Arousal Regulation Strategies*. Sports Psychologist, 8(3), 112–132.

Cumming, J., & Hall, C. (2019). *Imagery: The Looking Glass to Performance*. International Journal of Sports Psychology.

Davis, K., & Hollander, R. (2020). *Identifying and Managing Performance Anxiety among Young Athletes*. Journal of Sports Psychology.

Eklund, R., et al. (2021). *The Role of Goal-setting in Athletic Performance*. Journal of Applied Sport Psychology.

Gould, D., et al. (2019). *Youth Sports: Understanding the Nature of Psychological Challenges*. Sports Psychology Overview.

Smith, A. (2020). *The Impact of Performance Expectation on Youth Athletes*. Psychology of Sport and Exercise.

Côté, J., & Fraser-Thomas, J. (2007). *Youth and Sport*. In Psychology of Sport and Exercise.

Distefano, C., et al. (2018). *Communication and Team Dynamics in Sport*. Journal of Sports Sciences.

Gould, D., et al. (2008). *The Role of Youth Sports in Lifelong Development*. Sports Psychology Review.

Jones, M. V., et al. (2020). *Conflict Resolution in Youth Sports*. International Journal of Sports Science.

Smith, R. E., et al. (2019). *Peer Relationships in Youth Sports: Implications for Performance*. Journal of Sports Psychology.

Steffens, N. K., et al. (2017). *Social Identity in Team Sports*. Group Dynamics: Theory, Research, and Practice.

Tajfel, H., & Turner, J. C. (1986). *The Social Identity Theory of Intergroup Behavior*. In Psychology of Intergroup Relations.

Vallerand, R. J., et al. (2006). Collective and Individual Decision Making in Youth Sports. *Journal of Applied Sport Psychology*.

Baker, J., & Côté, J. (2003). From recreation to elite sport: A developmental framework for the acquisition of expert performance in sports. *Inquiries in Sport & Physical Activity*, 1(1), 23-29.

Côté, J., & Gilbert, W. (2009). An integrative definition of coaching effectiveness and excellence. *International Journal of Sports Science & Coaching*, 4(3), 307-323.

Fraser-Thomas, J., & Côté, J. (2009). Youth sports programs: An avenue to foster positive youth development. *Physical Education and Sport Pedagogy*, 14(4), 307-323.

Gould, D., Dieffenbach, K., & Moffett, A. (2006). Psychological characteristics and skills of successful elite Olympic athletes. *Journal of Applied Sport Psychology*, 18(3), 175-184.

Hastie, P. A. (2004). The impact of sport on the development of personal and social identities and sense of community. *Recreation, Park and Leisure Studies*, 3(2), 89-96.

Kelley, J. A. (2002). Gender and physical activity: A meta-analytical approach to understanding the impact of socialization on female athletes. *Journal of Sport Behavior*, 25(4), 393-414.

Tajfel, H., & Turner, J. C. (1986). The social identity theory of intergroup behavior. *In Psychology of Intergroup Relations*, 2nd ed. (pp. 7-24). Chicago: Nelson-Hall.

Weiss, M., & Chaumeton, N. R. (1992). Motivational orientations in sport. In J. G. McCarthy (Ed.), *Research Quarterly for Exercise and Sport*, 63(1).

Côté, J., & Strachota, J. (2009). Coaching and athlete development: A retrospective. *International Journal of Sports Science & Coaching*.

Eagly, A. H., & Wood, W. (1999). The origins of sex differences in human behavior: Evolved dispositions versus social roles. *American Psychologist*, 54(6), 408-423.

Gilbert, W., & Trudel, P. (2004). Analysis of coaching science. *International Journal of Sports Science & Coaching*.

Gould, D., Dieffenbach, K., & Moffett, A. (2006). Psychological skill training for complete performance. *The Sport Psychologist*, 20(1), 90-100.

Lehman, K. L., et al. (2021). Masculinity and mental health in young male athletes. *Journal of Sport Psychology in Action*.

McCarthy, P. J., et al. (2019). Gender differences in resilience among young athletes. *Journal of Applied Sport Psychology*.

McLean, S. A., et al. (2015). Body image and weight concerns in female athletes. *Sports Medicine*, 45(10), 1391-1408.

Möller, K. F., et al. (2017). Masculine norms and mental health in adolescent males. *Psychology of Men & Masculinity*.

Schember, T. A., & Boulting, N. (2011). Gender differences in competitive contexts. *The Sport Psychologist*.

Schmader, T., et al. (2007). Stereotype threat in academic and athletic domains: A review of the research. *Perspectives on Psychological Science*.

Bangsbo, J., et al. (2015). *The Impact of Role Models on Children's Sports Participation and Performance*. Journal of Sports Sciences.

Brackenridge, C. (2001). *The Role of Parenting in Youth Sport*. The Sports Psychologist.

Fletcher, D., et al. (2013). *Parental Expectations and the Development of Young Athletes: The Role of Support and Pressure*. International Journal of Sports Science & Coaching.

Gould, D., et al. (2006). *The Role of Parents in the Development of Young Athletes: A Multi-Factoral Perspective*. Journal of Sports Medicine.

López, F. (2010). *Pressure vs. Support: The Psychological Implications of Parenting Styles in Sports*. Psychology of Sport and Exercise.

Smith, R. E., & Smoll, F. L. (1996). *The Role of Parent-Child Relationships in Youth Sports: Theory and* Practice. Sport Psychologist.

Davis, S., Lee, H., & Zhang, J. (2022). The impact of mindfulness on the coping strategies of adolescent athletes. *Journal of Sport Psychology*, 34(2), 123-138.

Gould, D., Munz, R., & Jackson, S. (2019). Psychological factors in competitive sports: The role of anxiety and coping strategies. *The Sport Psychologist*, 33(1), 36-45.

Johnson, T., Harris, R., & Zhang, W. (2023). Evaluating the impact of mental health education programs in youth sports: A case study. *Youth Sports Research Journal*, 5(1), 19-34.

Keen, R., Smith, J., & Thomas, L. (2020). The relationship between mental health and athletic performance in adolescents. *International Journal of Mental Health and Sports*, 8(4), 201-212.

Purdy, K. G., Smith, T., & Johnson, R. (2021). Social media use and mental health outcomes in adolescent athletes: A systematic review. *Journal of Adolescent Health*, 69(5), 950-957.

Smith, L., Williams, M., & Bennett, C. (2020). How to balance sport and life: Recommendations for coaches and parents. *Sports Psychology Review*, 26(3), 204-219.

Zahra, F., Ahmed, S., & Qureshi, M. (2022). The role of coaches in athlete mental health: A review of literature. *Journal of Sports Coaching and Psychology*, 4(2), 101-112.

Dweck, C. S. (2006). *Mindset: The New Psychology of Success*. Random House.

Gould, D., & Udry, E. (1994). Psychological Skills for Enhancing Performance: Theory and Practice. *Applied & Preventive Psychology*, 3(4), 243-255.

Hinds, K. H. (2019). Building Resilience in Young Athletes: Effective Strategies for Coaches and Parents. *Journal of Sport Psychology in Action*, 10(1), 15-22.

Kreitzer, M. J., Seal, W., & Mo, J. (2018). The Effects of Mindfulness on Athletic Performance. *Journal of Sport and Exercise Psychology*, 40, 330-343.

Thelwell, R. C. (2013). The Role of Self-Talk in Sports Performance. *Journal of Sports Sciences*, 31(11), 1195-1203.

Yeager, D. S., & Dweck, C. S. (2012). Mindsets That Promote Resilience: When Students Believe That Personal Characteristics Can Be Developed. *Educational Psychologist*, 47(4), 303-314.

www.ingramcontent.com/pod-product-compliance
Lightning Source LLC
Chambersburg PA
CBHW072026040426
42447CB00009B/1747